House Rules
CLARE COULSON

BANTAM PRESS

LONDON · TORONTO · SYDNEY · AUCKLAND · JOHANNESBURG

TRANSWORLD PUBLISHERS
61–63 Uxbridge Road, London W5 5SA
a division of The Random House Group Ltd

RANDOM HOUSE AUSTRALIA (PTY) LTD
20 Alfred Street, Milsons Point, Sydney,
New South Wales 2061, Australia

RANDOM HOUSE NEW ZEALAND LTD
18 Poland Road, Glenfield, Auckland 10, New Zealand

RANDOM HOUSE SOUTH AFRICA (PTY) LTD
Endulini, 5a Jubilee Road, Parktown 2193, South Africa

Published 2005 by Bantam Press
a division of Transworld Publishers

A catalogue record for this book is available
from the British Library.
ISBN 05930 54547

Typeset in Minion

Printed at Clays Ltd, St Ives plc.

1 3 5 7 9 10 8 6 4 2

Papers used by Transworld Publishers are natural, recyclable products
made from wood grown in sustainable forests. The manufacturing processes
conform to the environmental regulations of the country of origin.

Contents

In memory of
Fiona Macpherson

Introduction

MOST OF US FANTASIZE about a domestic idyll where we sleep on heavenly smelling sheets and fluffy down-filled pillows and wake up to the sun streaming through sparkling windows. Where we bake cakes (deliciously light and sticky lemon ones) on a Saturday afternoon and friends come round in the evening and marvel at our delicious canapés and perfectly mixed Martinis. A stress-free life where everything is neat, orderly and in its place.

The reality, however, is that many of us don't know where to begin. There are people out there with top-of-the-range kitchens who have no idea how to cook a Sunday roast; there are some who spend hundreds of pounds on cashmere yet have no hope of washing it properly. There are others who cannot sew on a button, iron a shirt or unblock a drain. Shocking, isn't it?

You can, of course, get through life without knowing how to do all these things (although you will have to wear creased shirts with missing buttons) but knowing how to run your home with efficiency and style will radically improve your life. Getting dressed in the mornings is much easier when your clothes are washed and ironed and hung up, rather than thrown onto one big heap on the floor. Cleaning the bathroom takes no time at all if you whip round it every few days rather than waiting for the shower to become so mouldy that you simply can't bear it any longer.

This book is not a bossy-boots guide and I would be amazed, and a little horrified, if anyone followed all of the advice in these pages to the letter. It is a book for people who were probably never taught how to do these things when they were young and now find themselves in their twenties or thirties with an embarrassing lack of knowledge when it comes to the practicalities of life. But it's also a book for those people who are already clued-up but would love to delve a bit deeper or simply want to indulge their strange obsession with laundry sprays, pretty ironing-board covers and those gorgeous old-fashioned brushes that hang outside proper ironmongers. (Why are chores much more pleasurable when some fabulous-looking accessory is thrown into the equation?) It's a book to dip into, to find the answer to an occasional question, or to get inspiration for sorting out the airing cupboard, replacing lost buttons or throwing a glamorous *soirée*.

Everyone loves an insider tip, and this book is full of them, on subjects from mixing cocktails to ironing shirts, but anyone can pick up advice from experts if they use some savvy. Get into the habit of asking those-in-the-know for their advice too. In the middle of a pre-dinner-party baking flap, I have called a ritzy London restaurant to ask if it's OK to switch an ingredient in one of their recipes. They were incredibly helpful – especially considering that I was foolishly calling at about 7 p.m. when all hell was probably breaking loose in their steamy kitchen. I am not suggesting that you call the Ivy every night to ask a chef what to cook for dinner, but use a bit of initiative and don't be afraid to seek out a professional once in a while.

The knowledge gap when it comes to household management is a widely acknowledged fact. I have countless friends who, through little fault of their own, have a patchy knowledge of how their home works and invariably have to call their mother or a friend when they are faced with a domestic problem. But what happens to the people who don't have anyone to call upon, or to others who simply don't want to have to phone their mother-in-law (yet again) and admit defeat with the Yorkshire puddings? In an ideal world, we would all have a crack squad of experts to call upon, including a great cook who can offer reassurance when a Victoria sponge shows no sign of rising to the occasion, or a social butterfly who knows exactly what you should wear to a swanky evening wedding in the Highlands.

We all have some chores we enjoy doing and some we loathe, so the logical solution is to focus on the good stuff and try to minimize the bad, either by finding someone else to do it (first read the pointers on hiring help on page 122), or by dealing with it as quickly and efficiently as possible. No matter how saintly you are, sometimes life is too short to launder a houseful of linen sheets or take up the hems on a new pair of trousers. Knowing how to do everything is commendable but having the option to pick and choose exactly how much we want to do is a luxury; many of our mothers and grandmothers would not have been as indulged with the help and time-saving technology that make our lives so much easier today.

While knowing how to run your home is crucial (especially if you don't want to live like a slob or pay someone a fortune to do everything for you), it is just as important to create a gorgeous nest that makes you want to do the chores in the first place. If you are surrounded by things you love it will make all that cleaning seem a lot more worthwhile and, perhaps, even pleasurable.

When you do have to buckle down and get on with the jobs you hate, there are endless ways to make them more enjoyable: they simply need a little sugar-coating. This book will tell you how to do all the stuff that has to be done, but hopefully it will inspire you too; cleaning the bathroom seems less of a chore when there are lots of pretty glass decanters (full of delicious bath oils) to rearrange; and ironing isn't such a pain when you can listen to music (preferably on a peppermint-green Roberts Radio) and the finished product is a glorious set of clean sheets tied up with some striped ribbon. Treats are so important and their incentive value should never be underestimated.

It's not just at home that we are plagued by doubts about the right way to do things; there has never been more uncertainty about how to behave in some social situations. Where can you find the perfect house-gift for a weekend away with friends who appear to have everything? Is it acceptable to wear a strappy dress for the Royal Enclosure at Ascot? What on earth should you write in a condolence letter? This book will answer all these questions and more.

Living well is as much about knowing how to behave as it is about dealing with the mundane practicalities, yet even the simplest task, such as writing a thank-you letter, can throw the most able and practically minded among us into a mild panic. When I worked on a magazine, my first editor was old-school to the core, with immaculate manners and an unerring sense of what was right. Whenever she had been taken out to lunch or sent a gift she would always, without fail, send a beautifully written thank-you note in her signature brown ink on perfect white cards. Good manners take you a long way and a dash of charm will smooth the creases of life no end.

Making your daily existence more streamlined and less stressful is what this book is all about. It's not about torturing yourself with endless cleaning, washing, sorting and tidying. It's about making life easier and more enjoyable. Learning how to do things properly is important, and I hope that this book answers lots of questions, so that at the end of the week (or whenever) you can sit back, pour a big drink and relax, knowing that everything is as it should be.

Wardrobes

*How to care for clothes,
create calm and lead
a crease-free life*

FASHION ABUSE is a terrible thing but it's happening all around us and every one of us can be guilty of it. One minute those Manolo Blahniks are attracting admiring glances on the dancefloor, and the next they are back at home being tossed onto a dusty heap of sub-standard footwear where they will get creased and scuffed in no time at all. The Prada cashmere sweater you once worshipped from afar and spent a week's wages on – where is it today? All too often it's screwed up in a ball and stuffed in a dingy moth-ridden corner of your bedroom. And that Chloé jacket might look immaculate fresh from the shop but if it's cruelly hung on a metal coat-hook after its first outing it won't look good for long. There's no point spending a fortune on clothes if you don't treat them with respect.

Yet with good planning and careful organization, your wardrobe can become a temple in which your clothes are suitably enshrined. A well-ordered wardrobe is a joyous thing. Just imagine: open the door and a handy light switches on, illuminating your beautifully ordered possessions. Crease-free clothes are arranged according to type and colour, and hang elegantly from a uniform row of sturdy wooden hangers. Knitwear is folded and stacked on custom-made shelving, and shoes and boots are stored in box-sized pigeonholes. Belts, scarves, gloves and accessories are neatly arranged in drawers and there's handy storage space to pack away out-of-season clothes. The back of the door even has a full-length mirror, transforming your wardrobe into a virtual dressing room.

To anyone living in cramped urban conditions this might seem like a pipe dream but creating a similar sense of order and function within any space, no matter how Lilliputian, is the key to a blissfully ordered wardrobe where you can find everything in a flash. Learning how to look after your clothes, having them repaired promptly and treating them with respect, will keep them looking better for longer.

And it's not just about aesthetics; frantically searching for something to wear every morning is the last thing you need when you are late for work or madly trying to get to an appointment on time. If getting dressed takes you more than a few minutes then it's time to take action.

The complete wardrobe detox

As this is the beginning of a new relationship with your clothes, you need to make a fresh start. The best way to do this is to conduct a thorough, even ruthless, wardrobe detox. This is important because, as ludicrous as it sounds, there are clothes that are actually toxic. Their presence in your wardrobe can poison your self-esteem, cloud your judgement and, at worst, cause actual bodily harm to the clothes you really love to wear. Examples of toxic clothes include:

- Clothes that are past their sell-by date or haven't been worn for years. Learn to let go of the past.

- Vintage clothes that have not been decontaminated. They can be carriers for all sorts of nasties, including lethal moth larvae – the scourge of wardrobes everywhere.

● Impulse sale purchases that should have been left on the sale rail.

● Clothes you were planning to slim into. They are a constant reminder of failure, so get rid of them.

● Unwanted gifts. We all love our grannies but there's no room for sentiment in the wardrobe.

● Clothes left by ex-boyfriends.

● The trends that didn't translate. Some clothes were only meant for the catwalk.

The wardrobe detox is all about simplifying and, where possible, reducing the volume of your possessions. For most of us this requires a certain level of discipline. If you're a relentless hoarder then enlist a friend to help – someone strict, methodical and immune to your pleas to hold on to the dead wood of your wardrobe. This should also be someone whose style you admire and whose taste you can trust.

Separate clothes and accessories into piles by type and decide what you really need and what is simply using up precious space. With the exception of formal dresses or dinner jackets that might only get an occasional outing, apply a one- or two-year rule – if clothes have not been worn (or worse still, have not been seen) for this length of time, there's a good chance you will never wear them again. This is especially true of clothes bought because they were part of a fleeting trend.

When styles come back they rarely have the same cut or details, and that lime-green puffball skirt that was so cool in 1985 is never going to come back into fashion.

Classic pieces are more difficult to part with but apply the same rule: if they have languished for as long as you can remember, they should probably be banished. Keep reminding yourself of the space you will create and how serene your life will become with your clutter-free closet. A thorough sort-out will reveal old favourites you had forgotten about, as well as horrors you will be happy never to see again. The point is to create the order and space that will make getting dressed a pleasure, rather than a pain.

To make the whole process more enjoyable, make the effort to either sell or recycle unwanted clothes. Any rejects with a designer label can be taken to shops that sell good second-hand clothes and accessories, some of which (and this is the best bit) actually hand over cash on the spot for second-hand clothes – hard cash for your cast-offs. These shops tend to know what will sell so they might not want to take everything but don't be offended. You can donate the rest to friends or a charity shop, or recycle it at clothes recycling bins, which are found alongside some council-run bottle banks. Consider setting up an eBay account, too: see below.

○ DO allow enough time for a wardrobe detox. This is not a quick job but it's much better to do it in one sitting, so put aside at least one afternoon or a whole day.

○ DO play some upbeat music to make the process less painful.

○ DO try reselling. One man's trash is another man's treasure, and clothes and accessories in good condition, especially with a designer label, can make money.

○ DON'T double up on clothes. Once the contents of your wardrobe have been edited, you will be less likely to buy new clothes that you don't need.

USING EBAY

If you are reluctantly detoxing and find you have things that are too good to throw away or give away, try selling them on *www.ebay.co.uk*. You can sell pretty much anything to anyone on this hugely popular online auction site. Once discovered, eBay becomes totally addictive – seeing your cast-offs being snapped up by eager bidders is endlessly satisfying and it's incredibly straightforward to use. Once you have registered you simply attach an image of each item you are selling to the window and describe it as precisely and enticingly as you can. It is not compulsory to use pictures but it will help you to sell things and often at a higher price. Take digital images of everything you want to sell and make them look as appealing as possible. eBay

○ DO focus on the end result, stay focused and keep picturing your new streamlined closet.

Seasonal wardrobes

People who are very serious about their clothes religiously swap the contents of their wardrobes between seasons. So around April, winter coats, heavy suiting and thick knits will all be cleaned, repaired where necessary and packed away in boxes or trunks for the summer. To the uninitiated it might seem extreme but this is a routine that anyone can adopt.

☆ ☆ ☆ ☆ ☆ ☆ ☆ ☆ ☆ ☆ ☆ ☆

users can email questions to you but apart from answering them you simply wait for the auction to end, cash your payments and wait for them to clear, then post the goods (usually the buyer pays for postage and packing).

Having to check for messages, packing up parcels and taking them to the post office can be time-consuming but making money from things you would otherwise dispose of is a thrill and all in all the process is pretty painless. Do also check that you understand the costs as the website charges sellers for each listing and also takes a percentage from each sale; these costs can eat into your profits.

Another word of warning – buying on eBay is even more thrilling then selling, so try not to get carried away and spend all the money you have made.

☆ ☆ ☆ ☆ ☆ ☆ ☆ ☆ ☆ ☆ ☆ ☆

It protects clothes from moths and damp, and it creates space. If you are not going to wear those heavy four-ply cashmere polo-necks during the summer months, there is little point in letting them use up precious wardrobe space.

Whatever is going to be packed away needs to be properly cleaned and dried first. Never store clothes that have been worn, and don't put into storage clothes that have been sitting around getting musty for months on end, or you could later find them munched to pieces by moths. Once cleaned, clothes can be folded and wrapped in acid-free tissue paper and then put away somewhere safe; storage boxes or a clean, dry trunk are the safest and most practical places, although empty suitcases or sturdy cardboard boxes will do just as well.

Swapping over the contents of your wardrobe biannually is also a good opportunity to have a major clean. Everything should be removed, from neatly folded knitwear to the shoeboxes that congregate at the bottom of the wardrobe. Cleaning around things will not remove all the dust. Once the wardrobe is empty, clean the surfaces with the upholstery attachment of the vacuum cleaner and then wipe down all the surfaces with a damp cloth. Make sure that everything going back into the wardrobe is clean, too, especially if they have just come out of storage. Shoeboxes should also be given a wipe down, as they tend to collect dust even when they are stored away.

○ DO replace lavender bags or moth repellents when you edit seasonally. They usually lose their fragrance after a few months.

○ DO make sure that any boxes used for storage are totally mothproof. The wily creatures can squeeze into the tiniest nooks and crannies. Airtight containers or vacuum-packed bags are ideal. As long as clothes are totally clean and dry, they don't need to 'breathe'.

○ DO create enough space for your clothes to hang freely. Crushed clothes will simply need to be re-ironed before use.

The importance of proper hangers

Wire hangers are torture for your clothes. Fabric can develop permanent indentations from the wire, especially so in the case of knitwear and heavy jackets. When you get home with a stack of dry-cleaning, bin the wire hangers immediately so you are not tempted to use them. The only exceptions to this rule are shirts, although not if they are left hanging for long periods.

Smart wooden hangers are an investment. You will never have to replace them and if you shop around and buy in bulk they don't even need to be expensive. Padded hangers are essential for anything delicate that needs extra care, such as silk, velvet or beaded clothes. To protect vintage fabrics or decorated evening dresses, store them in hanging cotton garment bags, which are sold by the storage specialists overleaf.

Vintage expert Virginia Bates, who supplies super-models such as Kate Moss and Naomi Campbell with antique gowns,

STORAGE SPECIALISTS

Somehow just buying fantastic boxes can make the whole decluttering procedure much more enjoyable.

The Holding Company (020 8445 2888; *www.theholdingcompany.co.uk*). Expensive but extensive collection of great storage ideas, from deluxe leather boxes and chests which are useful for storing out-of-season clothes and could double up as side tables, to basic wicker or canvas boxes. There are also lots of novel wardrobe accessories, from innovative hangers and cedar blocks to mesh dress bags. As with Muji, the acrylic boxes are great for storing jewels and accessories too.

Morplan (0800 451122; *www.morplan.com*). This is where glossy magazines and many designers stock up on supplies, keeps very delicate pieces wrapped in tissue in card boxes, and sticks a Polaroid snap of the garment on the front of the box.

○ DO hang wishbone hangers in the same direction to save space.

○ DON'T hang delicate or vintage clothes where they can easily be snagged or damaged.

☆ ☆ ☆ ☆ ☆ ☆ ☆ ☆ ☆ ☆ ☆ ☆

from hanging bags, rails and hangers to bumper packs of acid-free tissue. To store precious things there are dress boxes in corrugated cardboard and breathable hanging bags for gowns or delicate pieces. Because it is intended for the trade, prices are competitive too.

Muji (020 7323 2208 for branches nationwide; *www.muji.co.uk*). Truly brilliant and highly addictive Japanese shop jam-packed with nifty storage from the best looking polypropylene or cardboard magazine files you can buy to a whole load of different boxes, including ones on castors that can roll under the bed. The acrylic stationery organizers can be used for storing jewellery, and the silicon ice-cube tray is the perfect receptacle for earrings or rings. Also fantastic bottles and tubs for decanting beauty supplies before travelling.

☆ ☆ ☆ ☆ ☆ ☆ ☆ ☆ ☆ ☆ ☆ ☆

○ DO avoid hangers that store several things at once. They are space-savers but they also encourage clutter and keep clothes out of view.

○ DO keep the number of padded hangers down. They are great for delicates but they are also bulky and use up space.

To hang or to fold?

The decision to hang or fold is often dictated by the amount of space available. If you are planning to reorganize your storage space, or even have something custom-made, it is worth considering that some things are always better folded while others should always be hung. Knitwear and clothes made from heavy, stretchy fabric can easily lose their shape when hanging and so are best folded. Anything delicate

---

☆

THESE CLOTHES SHOULD BE HUNG: coats; jackets; linen shirts, skirts and dresses; leather and suede; fur jackets and coats; silk or satin skirts and dresses; skirts with pleats; all suits; trousers with creases.

THESE CLOTHES SHOULD BE FOLDED: dresses that are delicate or beaded; jeans, cords and casual trousers; heavy knitted skirts; lingerie; scarves; sports clothes; sweaters and cardigans; T-shirts; heavy jersey or stretch fabrics.

and highly decorated, such as a beaded dress, is best kept folded, too, so it won't snag other clothes or get snagged. More structured pieces, such as tailoring, should be hung on good hangers.

Day-to-day clothes care

Clothes that have been worn and do not need to be washed should be aired at the end of the day before being returned to the wardrobe. If you've been in a smoky atmosphere for any amount of time, hang the clothes you've been wearing in a well-ventilated spot for an hour or two when you get back. Try not to leave clothes lying around where they will get crumpled and creased. It will require daily discipline but getting into good habits and hanging clothes up means they will always be ready to wear. And it's better than having to re-iron them at the last minute because they have been under a pile of other clothes for a week.

A clothes brush should always be on hand. A coat that's looking a bit dusty or crumpled will look much better once surface dirt has been removed. This also cuts down on trips to the dry-cleaner. Don't be too harsh in your brushing, however. Use the brush sternly enough to remove dust and always work with downward strokes so as not to upset the pile of the fabric.

When clothes return from being dry-cleaned, remove the plastic wrapping and leave them to air (by an open window if possible) before putting them in the wardrobe to allow dry-cleaning chemicals to evaporate.

○ DO leave invisible tailor's stitches sewn up in pockets on new coats and jackets. This will stop you putting your hands or anything else into pockets, which will help to retain shape.

○ DO spot-clean clothes after use to save on dry-cleaning bills.

○ DO clean clothes on the go. The mail-order catalogue Lakeland sells 'Sticky Mitts': individually wrapped sticky gloves that remove animal hairs, dirt and dust.

Repairs

Repairs should always be carried out as quickly as possible before the situation gets any worse. Small tears or loose seams can quickly develop into irreparable damage, and washing torn fabric will often cause more disrepair. If you don't have the time or inclination to do repairs, have them done by a local dry-cleaner or dressmaker. However, many repairs are simple enough to do at home with very basic knowledge. Sewing on a loose button takes a few minutes and is very easy, while trouser hems can be taken up in about an hour.

Keep a small sewing kit with some needles, pins, a sharp pair of scissors and some thread in neutral colours such as black, white and cream, as well as any other colours you might use. Some tailor's chalk is also useful but not essential.

Sewing a button

If a button is loosening, repair it as soon as you can. The button you lose is bound to be a unique vintage one that you can't replace. If the button has fallen off recently it will be obvious where it needs to be attached: you will see the indentation of the original stitches. If not, then mark the spot with a pin or chalk so you sew in the right place. Thread your needle, doubling the thread to make the stitches stronger. Knot the end of the thread, trim off any excess, then, before you attach your button, sew through from the wrong side of the fabric and back down to your starting point a few times. Then put your button in place and take the needle through the first hole of the button and back down through the next hole, looping back to your starting point. Repeat until the button is secure. If there are four holes you can criss-cross the stitches.

Once the button is firmly attached, sew the thread through the stitches on the wrong side of the fabric to secure it, then trim off excess thread. If attaching a button to thicker fabric, on a coat or jacket for example, be careful not to attach the button too tightly or there won't be enough space for the button to sit easily. Keep spare buttons in one jar or pin them to a utility-room noticeboard so that you don't lose them.

Sewing a hem

To hem trousers, a skirt or a dress you need only a few centimetres of fabric to turn up. If there is a lot of excess, it will need to be cut away. Pin the hem at the length you want the garment to be – for trousers either pin one leg and then match the opposite leg with a tape measure, or get a friend to pin for you while you are wearing them. Wear shoes while you are doing this or you could end up with trouser legs that are too short or too long.

Fold the fabric once and then again, and pin all the way. Then sew with a tacking stitch: work the needle loosely in and out of the fabric using a contrasting colour thread. This is simply to hold the fabric in place while you sew the hem properly.

Thread your needle with matching thread, knot the end and trim the excess, and begin by stitching through the folded edge of the hem: the part that won't be seen. Then pick up one barely visible thread from the reverse side of the fabric to hold the hem, before taking the needle back down into the folded edge. Take the needle back up again to repeat, so you are making a zig-zag line of stitches. No stitches should be visible from the right side of the fabric. Continue in neat, uniform stitches all the way around, then secure and trim the thread, and gently press the edge of the seam to create a sharper line.

Repairing a seam

Seams are better sewn by machine because machine-made stitches are stronger, but it's perfectly possible to repair a seam carefully by hand. Pin the fabric that needs to be sewn (with right sides together) and sew a tacking stitch all along to hold the fabric in place. Then, using matching thread, make tiny neat backstitches, taking the needle in and out of the line where the seam needs to be. To backstitch, the thread goes under the cloth for double the stitch length (apart from the very first stitch), and each new stitch is put in 'backwards' to meet the preceding stitch. The smaller the stitches, the stronger they will be, and the neater they are the less they will show on the right side. Continue until the seam is sewn and then do another couple of stitches at the end to secure the thread.

Knitwear care

Even the most sumptuous knits are not immune to problems, and the most common is pilling, where little balls of fibre develop around the sleeves of sweaters. Pilling is simply caused by friction so it's difficult to prevent, but it is quite easy to remove the balls of fibre using the small hand-held defuzzers or electric machines, sold at good department stores such as John Lewis.

○ DO store out-of-season knitwear safely to protect it from any damage.

○ DO hand-wash knitwear to keep fibres flat, which in turn will reduce the amount of pilling.

○ DON'T use pilling machines too often as over time they will wear away the fibres and thin the knit altogether.

○ DO get knits repaired promptly. The London-based **Cashmere Clinic** (020 7584 9806) can invisibly repair most tears and resuscitate old jumpers that are past their best.

If you have invested in cashmere from specialists you can go back to them for repairs. For a nominal fee **N. Peal** (see page 276) will mend, re-block and press their knitwear, no matter how old, to look as good as new. **Blossom & Browne's Sycamore Laundry** (see page 276) also offer a service whereby they will clean and return knitwear packed in tissue and ready for storage, which is worth using if you have no time to hand-launder your knitwear before packing it away for the summer.

Looking after shoes and boots

Shoes should last for years but they have to be treated properly. The biggest mistake you can make is to wear them every day, which means they never have a chance to dry out and are more likely to wear quickly and lose their shape. Always allow shoes to air-dry before putting them away, though never near a hot radiator, which will draw out leather's natural oils and could make shoes crack. The Holding Company has cedar 'shoe socks', small bags stuffed with cedar chips that help dry out shoes safely and keep them smelling fresh. Use wooden shoe trees to help maintain the shape of shoes. If the shoe tree feels tight it is probably about the right size: it will not stretch the shoe but will prevent creases forming.

Shoes and boots should be stored in boxes or on purpose-built shelves. If you leave them in disarray at the bottom of a wardrobe, they will lose their shape, get dirty and dusty, and are likely to inflict damage on each other, high heels being particular culprits. A wall of neatly stacked boxes will also take up less space. Plastic boxes will trap moisture so use card or canvas boxes, and to keep track of which shoes are in what box take a Polaroid snap of each pair (as most fashion editors do) and stick it to the front of the box – or just write a description. Finally, store the boxes away from heat, direct sunlight and damp.

Always get repairs done as soon as a problem is evident, if not before. Continuing to wear shoes once they are worn down causes greater damage to them. Soles can be ruined beyond repair, while allowing high-heeled shoes to wear down to the nail weakens the heel and could eventually break it altogether. Repairs should match the quality of the shoe. An elegant shoe with a fine leather sole will look heavy and far less beautiful once a thick rubber sole has been stuck to the bottom; a thicker sole also affects the delicate balance of the shoe and could even cause the heel to snap. Always bear this in mind when deliberating over what seem like costly repairs.

○ DO buy two pairs of your favourite shoes (and anything else you really love). It seems an indulgence at the time, but two pairs last more than twice as long as one pair because you are not tempted to subject a single pair to constant wear. You are also more likely to get repairs done on time.

SHOE WIZARDS

KG Shoes (020 7387 2234; *www.cobbler.co.uk*) has been in business for fifty years and carries out repairs for Gucci as well as the shoe departments of both Harrods and Liberty. As former shoemakers, the company has more expertise than you could wish for. They will take in or widen boots, repair surface rips and scratches on shoes and bags as well as rejuvenate and recolour the most battered shoes. Over one hundred shoes are repaired by post each week.

The girls at Jimmy Choo go to **Mayfair Cobblers** (020 7491 3426) to get their shoes and boots repaired, and customers post in accessories from as far afield as San Francisco and Singapore. The team will tackle anything from handbag and luggage repairs to shoes and boots in

○ DO stuff evening shoes with tissue after wearing them as this will help them to keep their shape and will also absorb excess moisture.

○ DON'T let a vast shoe collection, or any shoe collection for that matter, languish in a messy pile. Major shoe fanatics should invest in a custom-made shoe closet. Shoe minimalists should at least have a rack for sitting them on if they are not going to be kept in their original boxes.

☆ ☆ ☆ ☆ ☆ ☆ ☆ ☆ ☆ ☆ ☆ ☆

any material, although suede and leather is the speciality. They will also take in boots that are too big or stretch ones that are too small, and they provide a deluxe leather resole service, too, which is vital for delicate shoes.

It is hard to imagine anyone abusing their Manolo Blahniks but when they do they are sent to the **Chelsea Green Shoe Repair** (020 7584 0776) for rehab. They tackle everything from basic soles and heels through to repairs of rips and tears. The firm is especially good on delicate shoes, cutting heel tips to fit dainty stilettos and applying fine soles.

Do some local research too, as a good local cobbler is worth having in your address book. While they might not be able to perform miracles, they will extend the life of shoes and boots by fixing heels and soles, reattaching buckles and carrying out other small repairs.

☆ ☆ ☆ ☆ ☆ ☆ ☆ ☆ ☆ ☆ ☆ ☆

Cleaning shoes and bags

Leather shoes Leather shoe cream is the best thing to use. It is a natural product that will clean as well as keep the surface supple and shiny. Buy an established brand, such as Meltonian, in neutral, which contains no dye and can be used on any colour. Use only a small amount of cream and apply in small circular movements with a dry soft cloth before buffing the shoe with a clean soft cloth. Small marks on leather shoes and fabric can sometimes be removed with a rubber; gently rub the mark, which should eventually lift from the fabric. If brightly coloured leather becomes faded in certain areas, use an oil pastel (such as an artist might use) of the same colour over the affected areas, then top up with a neutral wax polish. Do buff leather soles – at Manolo Blahnik they advise gently rubbing the soles with fine-grade sandpaper to remove any surface dirt so the sole looks as good as new.

Suede and nubuck shoes Always treat new suede shoes with a waterproofing spray such as Scotchguard to protect against light dampness. Reapply regularly, although obviously you should try to avoid wearing the footwear in heavy rain. Once dry, suede and nubuck can be gently cleaned with a specialist brush (from shoe repairers); always move in the direction of the pile. Shoe designer Emma Hope advocates using steam to revive most suede and velvet shoes: brush off any excess dust or dirt, then hold the shoe over a steaming kettle. Stuff paper inside the shoe and leave to dry.

Silk, satin and other evening shoes Each time you wear them, wipe delicate shoes down with a soft cloth to take away dirt; use the upholstery attachment of the vacuum cleaner to lift dust from beading or embroidery. Stylists on fashion shoots often use a dab of lighter fuel to remove stains but it's always best to test a small area first, such as the inside of a heel, before tackling the problem in this way. Sandra Choi, Creative Director at Jimmy Choo, suggests using a Vanish stick to remove stains such as red wine or grass. Fill the shoes with lots of paper, dampen the stain slightly, then work in the stain remover with a soft toothbrush. It is unlikely to remove the stains completely but will usually lift off most of the mark.

Leather bags As with shoes and boots, a leather cream should be used to clean and moisturize bags. However, as materials vary widely, always check the best cleaning method with the shop when you buy a bag, or else test the cleaner on a small patch on the base of the bag and leave it for twenty-four hours before cleaning the whole thing. English bridle leathers contain lots of natural waxes which can rise to the surface causing a white 'bloom'. Use a piece of soft lint cloth to rub the leather and the bloom should disappear. When not in use, keep bags stuffed with paper to retain their shape and protect them from dust by storing them in felt bags; leather bags should be used often to keep them supple. If any leather bag gets soaked in a downpour, wipe away excess moisture with a soft cloth and let the bag dry out naturally, away from any direct heat. Have skins such as crocodile, alligator and snake cleaned professionally.

ACCESSORY STORAGE TIPS
from Lulu Guinness

IN AN IDEAL WORLD I would recommend putting handbags in their dustcover bags and storing them in a hat box so they can't be marked. However, I like to be able to see my handbags so I display them in glass-fronted cabinets in my bedroom.

VINTAGE BAGS also look pretty if they are hung like pictures on hooks on the wall. They look great all clustered together but they do tend to get a bit dusty!

YOU COULD ALSO BUY perspex cubes from shop-fitters, fill them with all your handbags and shoes and build them into a stack.

MY COLLECTION OF antique powder compacts is displayed under the glass top of a table. It's perfect: I can arrange them all as I like but they are kept safely under glass. Any other small accessories could be stored like this. I think it is such a shame to hide things away. I always try to display my favourite things so that I can see them every day.

Suede bags The treatment of suede bags should follow the same rules as for suede shoes (see above). Always treat suede regularly with a protector such as Scotchguard, but avoid getting the fabric wet wherever possible. As with shoes, suede bags can also be gently cleaned with a suede brush.

Evening bags After use, wipe down with a soft cloth. When not in use, wrap satin, velvet or beaded evening bags in acid-free tissue paper and store them somewhere absolutely dry and cool.

The enemy within – the clothes moth

Anyone who has had the misfortune to discover a prize possession munched to tatters by the moth will attest to the devastation they can cause in the wardrobe. Some homes, especially ones that are old, cluttered and stuffed with antique fabrics, seem to be an oasis for the moth, while others never come under siege from the relentless pests. Moths have expensive tastes: they feed on the proteins found in natural fibres, especially cashmere, wool and silk. They are also attracted to dirty clothes which could have traces of old food on them.

There is no cure for ravaged clothes. Prevention is the only answer and waging a wardrobe war is the only effective path to take. Cluttered spaces will simply provide additional shelter, so the first thing to do is to keep clothes and wardrobes scrupulously clean and tidy. Give wardrobes the equivalent of a spring clean between the seasons, removing everything and cleaning each nook and cranny. (For more on this, see page 15.)

The chemicals used in professional dry-cleaning will kill any larvae that might be invisibly setting up home in your cashmere sweaters, so dry-cleaning clothes before they are packed away is one solution. Boil-washing will also kill the larvae, which cannot survive extreme temperatures, although this is not usually an option with delicate clothes. Freezing them, however, will work just as well. Put clothes into watertight plastic bags and freeze them for about ten days, though first look out for anything that might crack in sub-zero temperatures, such as precious beads or buttons. Once clothes have been cleaned or laundered and dried, they can be wrapped and stored in acid-free tissue paper or, for the fanatical, in airtight bags, such as zip-locks, and put away for the winter.

One way to prevent moths is with natural deterrents, which are more pleasant to use than vile-smelling chemicals. Cedar is the most popular and you can buy it in blocks that

---

A FEMALE MOTH lays eggs for up to 3 weeks. The eggs hatch over a period from 4 to 21 days, after which the larvae start to feed for anything from 40 days to about 2 years, and they spin a web in which they will pupate. Pupation lasts between 8 and 44 days – then adult moths fly out of your wardrobe. Only the larvae feed on clothes so this is the danger period. Because the period is so long you have to deal with the problem really thoroughly, cleaning everything. If you leave just one piece of infested clothing, you can end up with your clothes being attacked once more.

either sit in the bottom of the wardrobe or hang from hangers. The Holding Company has a range of cedar wardrobe accessories, from Shaker-inspired hearts that hang with clothes to eggs that you nestle among clothes and larger hanging cedar blocks. You could even invest in a cedar chest to safely store out-of-season clothes. Lavender sachets and other spicy mixtures also help prevent moth invasions. Most boutiques now sell pretty versions that will scent your bedroom and help protect against moth damage. The level of defence you need does depend a little on your home: if you live in an old house that's not recently modernized or you've just had an infestation – or are in the habit of buying armfuls of vintage clothes – you will need something more powerful (and smellier) to keep the moths away.

◯ DON'T assume there are no moths because you haven't seen them. If you see one of the small, silvery, stealthy things it's usually too late – the larvae are what cause the damage.

◯ DO keep uncleaned vintage clothes well away from other clothes as they often carry harmful moth larvae. Always have vintage clothes cleaned before storing them.

Jewellery

Treat your jewellery well and it should last a lifetime, but store it badly and it is likely to scratch and wear very quickly. When it is not being worn, store it in suede or soft fabric pouches where it cannot be scratched or hit by other pieces. This is essential for pearls, which can very easily be damaged. A fabric roll is a good way to store jewellery and the best thing for travel: it takes up little space and keeps everything in perfect condition. If you have piles of sparkling costume jewellery you want to have on display, look for old-fashioned jewellery boxes, or use the clear perspex stationery drawers that are sold at shops such as Paperchase and Muji, which not only look great but also make finding everything much easier too.

Jewellery, especially if it isn't worn that often, will also need cleaning. Metals such as gold and platinum can be cleaned at home using a polishing cloth to remove small marks and scratches, but it should be taken back to the jeweller periodically for a more thorough cleaning. A good jeweller will offer a complimentary service for their own jewels. Society jeweller Asprey advises using an old, worn toothbrush to gently clean jewellery at home. Use warm water and a touch of washing-up liquid to remove any surface dirt and dust, rinse well and air-dry. But never use this cleaning method with coral, pearls or emeralds, which all need to be professionally cleaned. Pearls are probably the most needy jewels. They should always be stored in a suede pouch that is big enough not to strain the silk thread, and they will also need to be restrung professionally when required. Never spray perfume or hairspray near pearls because the alcohol will damage their nacre.

Your travelling wardrobe – how to pack a suitcase

Travelling puts clothes under stress. In the cramped conditions of your luggage, all the golden wardrobe rules are broken. Clothes are laid on top of each other next to shoes and boots, getting crushed and creased and dirty. Cases, more often than not, are crammed with snagging jewellery, exploding beauty products and messy creams. But you can avoid all these perils if you learn to pack properly. By packing well you can also make your travels much easier – the last thing any of us wants to do on a trip is whip out a portable iron or steamer and work through a pile of crumpled clothes.

The valets at Claridge's are probably as savvy as anyone when it comes to the art of packing. Some regular guests travel with up to sixty cases at a time, although Heaven knows what's actually inside all of them. The valets advise first arranging everything that is to be packed on a flat surface, such as a bed, and then putting similar pieces together. Not only can you see exactly what you have to pack, you can also see if there's anything you can do without. Almost all of us are guilty of overpacking. Maximizing the space you have is essential, and looking at everything before beginning to pack will help you make the most of every inch of suitcase space.

To pack like a professional, you need zip-lock bags and a pile of tissue paper. When clothes are wrapped in tissue it acts as a buffer zone against creases. Tissue can also be used to stuff the sleeves of coats and suits to keep them in better condition. Roll it into a sausage shape to stuff the sleeves of jackets, fold sleeves at the elbow where there will be a natural crease, then fold the jacket in half across the waist. Also use tissue paper to protect delicates from getting damaged in transit, and for all fabrics that crease very easily, such as silk, chiffon and linen. Thicker clothes travel much better, but beware of packing fluffy clothes next to anything at all. Mohair jumpers, pashminas and other knits have a habit of making everything else fluffy too, so wrap them in tissue first. Watch out for anything that could mark your clothes and do the same for them. If your shoes do not have their own felt bags, wrap them in tissue too. Fill empty shoes with smaller items such as socks or toiletries that have been wrapped well in sealed plastic bags.

Some people swear by rolling clothes, which is said to inflict fewer creases, while another school advocates folding. The only way to decide which you prefer is to experiment.

Arrange the heaviest things in the bottom of the case, evenly spread out so that the weight is distributed well. Forming a sturdy base like this will also help keep everything on top flat and more orderly. T-shirts, sportswear and jumpers can be rolled and used as padding for more delicate things, which should be packed close to the top of the case. Hats must always be stuffed well with tissue paper and surrounded with lots more, even if they are in hatboxes.

○ DO pack heavier items on the bottom of the case or bag, creating a firm base for more delicate things on top.

○ DO stuff tissue into sleeves and in between layers to reduce creases.

○ DO always wrap anything that could leak in secure plastic bags. Even if the lids are tightly screwed on, the pressure on flights has an unpredictable effect on anything that seemed otherwise perfectly secure.

○ DO unpack as soon as possible on arrival and hang creased clothes in a steamy bathroom.

○ DO have precious jewellery insured before travelling. When jeweller Solange Azagury Partridge went to a wedding in the South of France with a stack of diamonds, she ended up wearing them every day, having forgotten to get them insured. While diamonds on the beach might look quite chic and catch the light nicely, it is always wise to insure anything this precious.

○ DON'T check jewellery in with your luggage when travelling. If your cases get lost, at least you will have the most precious things with you.

The
Bedroom

*The fundamentals for
a blissful night's sleep*

THE BEDROOM IS WHERE we begin each day, recharged after a heavenly night's sleep. It's where most of us (those of us without dressing rooms, at least) prepare to face the world. It's the place we don't want to leave in the morning and the only place we really want to be when we are exhausted, sick or feeling sad. The bedroom needs to be somewhere we feel cosy, cosseted and blissfully relaxed, so it makes sense that this room should be the pinnacle of gorgeousness in your home, adorned with things you love and want to be surrounded by.

Ideally the bed should be a joy to sleep in, not lumpy and bumpy and inherited from unknown previous owners. It needs to be kept deliciously fresh and welcoming, and as we all sleep very differently, it needs to have the right pillows and bedding for you – it's no good piling your bed with deep feather-filled pillows if you are plagued by allergies. Equally, there's no point in styling your bedroom like a magazine photo shoot with piles of coordinated cushions, bolsters and pillows if making your bed in ten seconds flat is your priority.

Bedrooms need to be calming and streamlined, but instead they can quickly become a dumping ground for all the stuff that doesn't have a home elsewhere. Clutter will keep dust levels up and house a million tiny mites invisible to the human eye (as well as a few more visible ones too), and will make your surroundings much less inviting. By introducing methodical storage you will have a clutter-free, dejunked space and a cleaner, clearer atmosphere that will help you to wake all the better after eight hours' sleep. A soothing retreat will be easier to create if there are few reminders of the chaos of the outside world.

Bedroom basics

Does anyone open windows any more? Our grandmothers would have flung open their bedroom windows, and all other windows for that matter, every morning to ventilate stuffy rooms, and they invariably pulled back bedding at the same time to give beds a good airing, too. Gusty breezes will freshen rooms, chasing out any toxins, drying out dampness in the atmosphere and removing from bedding the moisture that unavoidably builds up while we are sleeping (gruesome fact: we lose up to a pint of moisture each night). It also helps to keep nasty pests at bay – there's nothing that microscopic creatures like more than cosy, damp, dark nooks and crannies in which to feast and multiply. These age-old rituals are not so easy to maintain these days when open windows are more likely to let in stealthy burglars than fragrant breezes, but a little ventilation is always better than none at all. Even if time is tight in the morning, try to open the windows and pull back bedding while you are getting ready for the day ahead. Even half an hour of fresh air circulating around your bedroom will make a difference. Turn back duvets, bedding and blankets every morning so that moisture has a chance to evaporate from the bed. Ideally you should leave the bed to air all day, but coming home at the end of the day to an unmade bed is not an uplifting experience, so if you prefer make the bed and tidy up just before leaving for work.

At weekends, when time might not be at such a premium, try to leave the windows open all morning and strip the bed at the same time so that the mattress is given a good airing, too. Get into the habit of doing this on a weekly basis when you are changing the bedding. If your bedroom is clutter-free, cleaning will be easy. You should only need a quick whip-round with a duster and the vacuum cleaner once a week. The biggest problem in the bedroom will probably be dust, so when you have time for a more thorough clean, try to get into every nook and cranny where dust may lurk. Run a soft brush or the upholstery attachment of your vacuum cleaner over the mattress and base to collect dust and fluff. This will also help to prevent dust mites. Always do this with the windows flung open. Don't forget to vacuum under the bed, pulling it away from the wall if necessary, to get rid of dust build-up. If you have storage under your bed, take everything out and vacuum around all the edges and skirting, and then clean storage boxes thoroughly before replacing them.

○ DO change bedlinen at least once a week.

○ DO use lightly scented detergent on bedlinen to leave a soft aroma rather than the heavy, soapy smell some commercial brands have.

○ DO use your bed for sleeping, not brunching, lunching or, heaven forbid, late-night takeaways. Breakfast in bed, especially hunks of toast dripping in butter and jam or flaky croissants, should be limited to special occasions such as lazy Sunday mornings.

    ○ DON'T come home from work and collapse
straight on to your bed. Have a shower or bath first,
put on clean nightwear and then snuggle up under
your duvet.

Sleeping well

Anyone who has spent more than a few nights unable to sleep
knows how debilitating and depressing it can be. If you collapse into bed and fall asleep straight away every night, you
are truly blessed – the rest of us need all the help we can get.
Make sure that your room is aired well, as fresh air is con-
ducive to sleep, and, if possible, leave your window open at
night (though in a basement flat in a crime-ridden area this,
quite obviously, is not viable). A temperature of around 24°C
is the best for sleeping, so don't keep heating on through the
night or sleep under duvets or blankets that are too thick.
Check that your mattress and pillows are right for you. These
strongly affect how you sleep.

    If your mind is racing after a stressful day or you are pre-
occupied or worried, getting to sleep will be even harder. Turn
on a light and make a list. Either a to-do list so that you don't
have to worry about remembering things, or simply write
down whatever is bothering you – getting whatever concerns
you have onto paper in black and white does seem to remove
them from your mind.

    ○ DO avoid turning your bedroom into an office.
It is fine to read something light at night to help

you get to sleep, but spending time in bed doing anything too mentally stimulating is likely to keep you awake.

○ DO get up and do something for twenty minutes if you've woken up and cannot get back to sleep. Browsing through cookbooks is a great way to spend the early hours of the morning. They are easy on the eye and deeply relaxing.

○ DO get into the habit of having an aromatherapy bath at night if you suspect you are going to find it difficult to get to sleep. The best of these work wonders.

○ DO try to avoid screens in the bedroom – televisions, computers and other similar electrical equipment are best kept in a different area if possible.

○ DO take a herbal sleeping tablet when all else fails. Valerian is amazingly potent, while kava kava is a gentler alternative (but avoid both if you are pregnant). Good bedtime herbal teas are camomile, lime blossom and valerian.

○ DO install soft, gentle lighting, avoiding strong overhead lights in favour of glowing bedside lamps and uplighters.

○ DO get up at the crack of dawn if you are wide
awake. It is absolutely the best time for getting all
your chores done with no distractions.

Duvets and pillows

Let's start with the best – which, of course, you should always
aim for if you can afford it. Paying hundreds of pounds for a
duvet seems like a ludicrous thing to do, especially when there
are much cheaper serviceable alternatives, but if your bed is
the centre of your universe, the most indulgent, luxurious
bedding is going to be a treat worth splashing out on. The very
best hand-plucked Siberian goose-down duvet from John
Lewis (which is, incidentally, a great one-stop shop for bedding) has the fluffiest down, offering optimum warmth at the
same time as being incredibly lightweight. The most highly
prized duvets have natural fillings, which generally give the
most warmth for the least weight. Goose has softer, warmer
down than that of other birds, so duvets made from goose-
down are the fluffiest and cosiest of all. More economical
duvets have a higher percentage of feathers over down.
Natural down and feather pillows are long-lasting and will
mould around your head; they are available in different combinations to provide a range of choice, from firm full pillows
to soft, giving ones. Similarly, pillows are available in synthetic
as well as natural fibres. It is definitely worth taking time to
choose the right firmness of pillow for you as this can radically affect how well you sleep.

While they might not sound quite so luxurious, synthetic duvets are now designed to be as close to natural materials as possible, offering lightweight yet warm fillings, the most expensive of which will have the finest polyester fibres and casings. Synthetics are preferable for anyone with allergies.

○ DO use the right duvet for each season. The warmth is measured in togs ranging from 3 to 13.5, with the lowest a light summer weight between 3 and 4.5 and the highest a thick winter weight up to 13.5. Buy a combination duvet, where two duvets button together, to have the best of both worlds.

○ DO buy your duvet a size bigger than your bed. It will look better when the bed is made and is much cosier to wrap up in.

○ DO have duvets and pillows professionally cleaned from time to time – it is much easier than trying to clean them at home. All naturally filled duvets and pillows will need to be professionally cleaned.

○ DO protect your mattress with a special cover that can also be regularly cleaned. It is a good idea to protect pillows with covers, too.

○ DO turn your mattress every quarter so that it wears evenly.

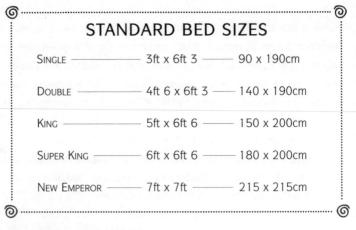

STANDARD BED SIZES

SINGLE	3ft x 6ft 3	90 x 190cm
DOUBLE	4ft 6 x 6ft 3	140 x 190cm
KING	5ft x 6ft 6	150 x 200cm
SUPER KING	6ft x 6ft 6	180 x 200cm
NEW EMPEROR	7ft x 7ft	215 x 215cm

Buying bedlinen

People can get terribly precious about their sheets, boasting rocketing thread counts and embroidery hand-sewn by legions of Italian peasants. The most highly prized bedlinen by famed producers such as Frette and Pratesi can cost thousands of pounds. A chic new hotel would not dream of opening its doors these days without the mandatory designer bedclothes, and a pop diva wouldn't sleep in anything less. The fineness of a bed sheet is measured by its thread count (the combination of warp and weft threads), which is an indicator of how finely woven the fabric is. So the very finest Italian linen has a thread count of up to 500, a more basic Egyptian cotton sheet will have a thread count of around 200, while good old poly-cottons are generally around 144. Yet thread counts, which can be misleading because they are only a measure of quality when referring to plain weave fabrics, are not the only thing to consider when buying sheets.

Natural fabrics are better because they 'breathe' and are thus healthier for us. Simple cotton sheets are the most economical, though Egyptian cotton has stronger, finer threads. It's important to think about laundering, too. While good linen sheets are generally considered the most covetable, they require more care than basic sheets – they need to be carefully laundered and rigorously ironed. Cotton irons much more easily and is a good deal easier to care for, while poly-cotton sheets are the most crease-free of all, though some do not wear as well over time as pure cotton.

Sets of simple white bedlinen are probably the best investment. Like neutral decoration, plain white sheets are classic and totally versatile; they go with virtually any colour scheme and can be dressed up with throws and cushions to change the look of your bedroom. Unless you want to spend hours styling your bed each morning, avoid endless coordinated cushions and throws, which look appealing when photographed in glossy magazines but are just plain annoying in real life.

○ DO steal ideas (not products) from good hotels – their decorators have traipsed around the world hunting down the fluffiest pillows and duvets and the very best bedding. Many hotels now actually sell their sheets too.

○ DO tie sets of pillowcases and sheets together with ribbon after washing so that they are always in a complete set when you need to find them.

○ DO always check the care labels on decorated sheets before buying.

The basics of bedlinen

Flat sheet Can be used as the bottom layer of the bed and/or the top layer for a traditionally made bed with blankets. As a bottom layer it needs to be properly tucked in, preferably with hospital corners, which means pulling the sheet tight and folding it carefully around each corner of the mattress as though you were wrapping a parcel, rather than scrunching it up and shoving it underneath. This neat stretching and folding gives you a securely fitted sheet, with a pleasingly smooth top surface.

Fitted sheet A base sheet that has elasticated corners that are easily and quickly pulled down around the corners of the mattress, with no tuck-in required.

Valance A cosmetic sheet, usually with a gathered skirt, that hangs over the base of the bed to conceal the divan.

Duvet covers Can be fastened with zips, ties, poppers or buttons. Buttons and ties are the most practical option as they can be easily replaced or resewn when they come loose, while zips and poppers could require professional mending.

Oxford pillowcase A standard case with a cosmetic border that is normally used for the top pillow.

BEDROOM TIPS

from Kelly Hoppen

LAYER lots of contrasting textures; this gives a very sensual feel to the room. 'Tactile' is the key word in the bedroom: bedding, throws, upholstery, carpets, curtains. Combining cashmere and linen with satin on a bedcover or cushions is a great way to achieve this.

KEEP COLOURS muted with a very neutral palette. I always paint bedroom walls with colours from my Perfect Neutral range.

WHITE EGYPTIAN COTTON sheets are essential to my bedrooms; after all, these come in direct contact with your skin all night, so go for the best quality.

LIGHTING is important in your home but especially so in the bedroom, I think. It's great to get different setting possibilities, which means you can dim the lights if you want to make the room more relaxing, and brighten them if you want to read or put your make-up on.

HAVE REGULAR CLEAROUTS and adapt your room to the seasons. There are many ways you can do this. Change the bedcover, cushions and blinds to lighter textures in summer, and use heavier, more luxurious fabrics in winter.

Square pillowcase A basic pillowcase with no border.

Pillow cover Used to protect the pillow before it is put inside the pillowcase. It will also keep pillows fresher and cleaner and can be removed easily for washing.

Mattress cover A protective cover that will provide an extra layer of warmth and protect the mattress from getting dirty, as well as prolonging its life.

Lounging kit

Remember the bedroom is sacred ground. You should never stomp around here in your outdoor shoes. Have a wonderful pair of slippers to change into or simply pad around in your bare feet; it will keep your home cleaner and it sets a more relaxed tone. Cosy clothes and luxurious throws are essential for lounging too, whether you are keeping snug during dark winter nights or watching the rain (or Cary Grant movies) on stormy Sunday afternoons.

Start with a vast fluffy throw. Department stores such as John Lewis and House of Fraser have some of the best, made from insulating wool and cashmere through to lighter cotton versions for spring and summer (buy a size bigger than your bed for added comfort). **Brora** (*www.brora.co.uk* or 020 7736 9944) also has cashmere blankets in gorgeous stripes as well as cashmere dressing gowns and soft, stripy bed-socks, while **Toast** (*www.toastbypost.co.uk* or 0870 240 5200) is another good catalogue for cocooning clothes, from pampering pyjamas and dreamy dressing gowns to chunky bed-socks and slippers, all with a slightly Nordic feel. Another irresistible source of nesting kit is **hush** (*www.hush-uk.co.uk*) which has everything from fleecy pyjamas and angora throws to rich Spanish drinking chocolate. There are even reading suggestions and recommendations of the perfect films to watch while nesting in style.

Storage

As the most private room in our home, the bedroom can become a dumping ground for anything with no obvious abode. Old copies of magazines congregate in corners, piles of books already read or waiting to be read mount up and shelves groan with cosmetics and products hoping one day to be used. If you want to create a relaxing, restful room glowing with feng shui goodness, streamlining is essential. In the same way that your wardrobe should undergo a seasonal detox (see page 19), so should your bedroom. To get started you will need to devise a system that is as ergonomic and unobtrusive as possible. The best and most expensive option is bespoke storage (wardrobes, shelving, drawers and boxes), preferably made by a highly recommended and mind-blowingly efficient carpenter. If you plan to stay in your home long term, and especially if you have tricky areas to fill, custom-made storage is certainly worth the expense.

Taking the bespoke route means that you will obtain the maximum amount of storage for the space you have, including alcoves or areas with sloping roofs. Visit a storage specialist, such as Californian Closets (see page 274), for help with a custom-designed scheme, or for a DIY approach go to Ikea where they sell a range of cavernous wardrobes with a multitude of options for rails, baskets, drawers and so on.

When you plan storage, think about what you may need in the future, not simply what your needs are right now, and don't despair if you can't afford new furniture: there are lots of ways in which you can create more storage by simple tricks. Just remember the golden rule that whenever space is at a premium, storage needs to be as multi-functional as possible.

Storage ideas

Chests are great for storing out-of-season clothes, extra bedding and blankets. To keep moths away either use a cedar chest or add some cedar blocks or other natural moth repellent. The Holding Company's Bout de Canapé, which looks like an antique travelling chest, could also double-up as a bedside table, while antique chests (which are easy to find at regional auction houses) look lovely, but make sure that they are totally dry before using them for storage, and if necessary line them with some beautiful floral wallpaper, too. Chests at the foot of the bed can double-up as a little seat, and old-fashioned ottomans

also offer hidden storage opportunities. Rather than simply having an ordinary table next to your bed, choose something with storage space underneath, even if it's simply used as a shelf for books.

Always make the most of the useful space underneath your bed, but make sure that whatever you use is easily movable so that the area is easy to clean and dust. Wooden boxes or even old drawers can be put on wheels (which you can find in DIY stores) and used as under-bed storage: make sure you allow for the height of the wheel and add some inches for clearance too. See-through plastic boxes (with lids) are brilliant for storing anything because you can see at a glance what is inside. Muji and Ikea both have neat versions of these; they are very easy to keep clean too. If you are using cardboard boxes or anything else opaque, give each one a label listing the contents to make it easy to locate whatever you need. Finally, if your bedroom is very small, think about having your bed raised so you can fit in more storage underneath it; the higher you go the more space you will have, and a high bed is quite dramatic in a Princess and the Pea kind of way.

Once you have your satisfying new storage, you must avoid the temptation to fill it up with clutter. The most crucial aspect of dejunking is getting rid of all the stuff you don't need or use. Get into the habit of having regular culls because clutter can gather at great speed and with alarming ease. Decluttering means you can find things more easily and it creates a cleaner, healthier room that's a doddle to tidy and more relaxing to spend time in. Don't simply move everything from one place to another or put it out of sight temporarily. You will need to spend a day thoroughly sorting everything and deciding what you need to keep, and you must be tough about this. Allow yourself to keep only a few things for sentimental reasons, and store them all in a special box.

○ DO discipline yourself not to buy things that will clutter up your life even more.

○ DO tear out pages from magazines that you want to keep and file them. These will take up much less space than piles and piles of back issues. (But don't throw away first copies or collectable magazines – they are sometimes worth hundreds of pounds.)

○ DO set up an account at *www.ebay.co.uk* and sell anything you don't use (see page 18). Designer clothes and accessories sell brilliantly.

○ DO throw away any perfumes and unused make-up that is more than a year old. Or donate them to a young daughter, niece or goddaughter, who will probably love them for her dressing-up box.

Guest bedrooms

Organizing guest rooms for visitors is the fun part of having your nearest and dearest to stay. If they will be sleeping in a spare room or guest room that's not used very often, you should spend a night there yourself to make sure it's not freezing cold or thoroughly uninhabitable. Rooms that are left empty can quickly become cold or damp or develop strange noises you are normally unaware of. Of course, if you are a paragon among hosts, you may well give up your own cosy bedroom, but if not, do make sure that you have made your guest room as comfortable and inviting as possible. Remove any clutter that is lying around to create a neutral, welcoming environment.

Make the bed with bedlinen that has been laundered with nice detergent and perfectly pressed with lavender water to make it smell heavenly, and ensure that the bed will be warm enough (a hot-water bottle in a soft cover is a real treat). Provide extra pillows as well as some cosy throws or blankets, which will also make the bed look more welcoming. If girlfriends are coming it's fun to fill their room with gorgeous treats. Light a scented candle before guests arrive so that the room is fragrant. Adapt this to whoever you have staying, so use light florals for a feminine fragrance or woody, spicy scents for a more masculine atmosphere. Lay out a cosy robe – it's the one thing that always seems too bulky and indulgent to pack. Leave some chunky socks out, too, for padding around in the morning. It's also thoughtful to provide a bottle of water, a bedside lamp that works and something interesting to read – you can tailor this to whoever is staying. Hangers are often overlooked but are invaluable, and a radio will make the room feel more lived in. Try to make it a home from home – a sort of mini boutique hotel with lots of personal touches.

Bedrooms away from home

Sleeping in hotel rooms can be Heaven or Hell. The best ones make you feel as though you are at home, only with much better bedding and accessories, while the worst make you wish you were still at home. When you travel, take a few customizing essentials to ensure that you sleep well in your temporary surroundings. Travel candles are great for making alien rooms smell more like you want them to. Red Flower mini candles come in delicious and fresh floral fragrances, such as American Lilac and Indian Jasmine, and they have their own miniature matches, too. L'Artisan Parfumeur's travel candles are also excellent, while the Body Shop do scented tea-lights that are light to pack. Take throws or large wraps, which are must-haves for travelling in any case, and use them as throws to soften up hotel chairs and beds. If you are worried about the bed or the sheets you are sleeping in (which is likely if, for example, you are roughing it), take precautions. I know one particularly luxury-loving fashion designer who packs his own silk sheet folded in two and sewn up the side to act as a barrier between himself and below-par bedding. This opulent sleeping bag packs down to virtually nothing.

The Bathroom

Soaking in style and the clinical clean-up

BATHROOMS ARE NO LONGER purely functional, clinical-looking spaces. They can be luxurious rooms where we soak for hours on end, reading a brilliant book or the latest issue of *Vogue*; where we create faux spas applying all the latest masks or grooming until every stray eyebrow is plucked to perfection. As such, they not only need to be meticulously organized and as ergonomic as possible, but also packed with everything to make our bathtime experience indulgent and languorous, or, when time is short, simple and streamlined. Striking the right balance is straightforward as the bathroom is a room with very little in it – or, at least, it should be. Hotel bathrooms are utter bliss not just because someone else picks up the towels and makes the sink gleam, but because they are pared-down and simplified.

As with every other room, decluttering the bathroom is essential and planning the appropriate storage should be a priority. Once the room is clear of clutter, cleaning it should be a breeze. Even if your bathroom is utterly basic, there are easy ways to transform it into a spa-like space with simple organization and accessories. Piles of fluffy towels, big beautifully lit mirrors and gorgeous products will turn what can be a mundane space into a calming hideaway where you can lock out the rest of the world.

Organization and storage

There are things you want to have on display in the bathroom, and things you really don't, so storage needs to be a mixture of closed and open. First, take a serious look at what you keep in your bathroom. Toiletries, cosmetics and bath products can quickly multiply and take up valuable space so look objectively at the endless bottles, tubes and tubs and decide which you actually use. Anything that has been unused for the last six months should go straight into the bin or, in the case of outrageously expensive products, donated to a friend who will appreciate them. As well as making it easier to find whatever you need, minimizing clutter in the bathroom will make it a more relaxing space, and make it easier to clean – old products left out in the open collect dust and look messy.

Decide which things you use most and store them near to where you use them (bath oils next to the bath and so forth). If bath products are beautifully presented, leave them on display; those in humdrum packages can be poured into decorative decanters. Glass jars, with or without lids, are a great way to store all sorts of things in the bathroom. Larger ones can be filled with scented colourful soaps (look out for loose soaps in old-fashioned chemists or at markets when you are on holiday – Provence is a great place to buy them in bulk), while smaller ones make good receptacles for cotton wool or cotton wool buds. Both the White Company and the Holding Company sell these jars via mail order, and department stores such as John Lewis are also good hunting grounds.

Larger things such as fresh towels or loo rolls can be stored in baskets, although in bathrooms where the users splash around you will have to use a lid. If your space is limited, then install shallow cupboards or shelving. As well as taking up less space, this will also discourage you from hoarding old products, which can easily get lost in a wasteland of bottles when cupboards are deep. In larger cupboards, group different types of products together. If you have a huge bathroom and you want to create an opulent vintage-look room, you could install an armoire where everything from towels and loo rolls to toiletries and a cleaning kit could be stored. Buy one at a local auction, where this kind of bulky furniture usually goes for a song, but check the feasibility of getting it into your home first. If your bathroom really is that big, why not add a huge squishy armchair too so that you can hold court while luxuriating in a tubful of bubbles and your audience has somewhere to sit?

○ DO save space by installing a mirrored cupboard above your sink.

○ DO store towels away from bath and basins or anywhere they could get damp – up high is probably best. Alternatively, store them out of the bathroom in a warm airing cupboard or other nearby area.

○ DO buy new toiletries only when the old ones have run out or are just about to, rather than cluttering cupboards.

Towels

An endless supply of big, fluffy towels is one of the best things about a luxurious bathroom, but having the right towels is also important. Good quality, thick towels will not only last

HOME SPA TIPS

from Marcia Kilgore, Founder of Bliss Spa

SWAP bulblight for candlelight.

PLAY a Shirley Horn or Carmen McCrae CD.

BLEND some essential oils into your bathwater (lavender, mint and rosemary make a fabulous mix) or sprinkle in some fresh rose petals for added spa sensation.

SPEND at least 20 minutes giving yourself a pre-soak body scrub (just the time you take will make you feel pampered).

PUT your fluffiest pillow behind your head (wrap a small hand-towel round it to stop it getting wet).

ENSURE a tub-side supply of red wine (for its anti-oxidant qualities) and brownies (for their serotonin-releasing ability) to maintain continuity between physical and mental states of relaxation.

APPLY a mask pre-bath – the steam will help the active ingredients penetrate more effectively into the skin.

WHEN you step out of the tub, apply your body moisturizer to still-damp skin, so the active ingredients and humectants can soak into the skin for longer-lasting, more-substance moisture.

longer but also provide a more decadent bathroom experience, so they are worth the investment. You will, after all, get the benefit from them every single day, and cheaper towels can be a false economy because they wear more quickly and can fade too. Just like sheets, towels are graded by their weight. The best towels have a deeper pile and are more absorbent – making them more efficient as well as more luxurious.

You should look for a deep pile, but don't be seduced by the biggest, thickest towels available. They require more storage space, and take for ever to dry, which, if you tumble-dry, means they will be twice as expensive to care for. Egyptian cotton towels are, along with Turkish-made ones, the most coveted: they are stronger and have longer fibres, making them fluffier and more absorbent without undesirable bulk.

When buying towels, your decisions will, of course, be led by your personal taste, but do think about the practicalities. Bright and colourful towels might tempt you, but white or neutral colours are by far the easiest to care for, and, like a plain bathroom, can provide a neutral backdrop for more

TOWEL SIZES

BATH SHEET —— 100 x 150cm

BATH TOWEL —— 140 x 70cm

HAND TOWEL —— 90 x 50cm

GUEST TOWEL —— 50 x 30cm

FACE CLOTH —— 30 x 30cm

colourful bathroom accessories. Avoid towels that have a silky finish, which makes them less absorbent. Beware, too, of intricate detailing which can be tricky to launder. Vast bath sheets can seem appealing in the shop and are great for cocooning but they are not the most practical shape and are bulky to store. Bath towels are a more manageable size and are easier to fold and store, while hand towels are the perfect size for drying hair as well as hands.

To keep bathrooms looking as streamlined as possible, install a rail for towels. A heated rail is a real indulgence that will not only keep your towels dry and warm but keep the room cosy too. Otherwise look in antique shops for Victorian wooden rails, which will help keep towels from ending up in a damp pile on the floor.

○ DO wash new towels before using them. It will take a few washes for them to de-fluff and at this stage they should only be washed with other similarly coloured towelling.

○ DO put underwear into a bag or pillowcase if they need to go in the same wash as your towels, as the metal hooks on bras can pull and rip the loops on the towel. Better still, protect towels by washing them separately.

○ DO soften the water in your washing machine with a handful of soda crystals – hard water can make towels go grey.

○ DO wash sets of coloured towels at the same time so they fade equally. If there is a dramatic fade, then take them back to the shop.

○ DO avoid using fabric softener in every wash. Used occasionally it will soften the towelling but used too often it will coat the towel and make it less absorbent.

○ DO use a mild detergent. It will be kinder to skin and won't leave towels with a nasty artificial smell.

AQUIS TOWELS

ONCE YOU'VE DISCOVERED Aquis towels, you'll find them indispensable. For anyone with long locks they are a godsend. More like a chamois leather than a normal towel, they are made from microfibre instead of cotton loops and absorb water at a much quicker rate, radically reducing hair-drying time. They are also lightweight, take up less space than normal towels and dry out more quickly too, making them perfect for travelling and holidays. You can buy them by mail order from **Space NK** (0870 169 9999), **Bliss Spa**, where it's called the Super Hair Shammy (020 7584 3888), and many regional department stores such as **Fenwick** (020 7629 9161).

Mirrors

Installing a well-lit mirror is likely to make a big difference to how functional your bathroom is. Make-up artists know how to work a mirror. James McMahon, who paints the faces of models such as Sophie Dahl, says that the ideal is a mirror hung in front of a window where there is natural daylight. A backlit mirror, where the light source is even, is good if you have no windows in the bathroom, but a light source that hits the mirror from above or from either side creates shadows across your face. It is worth considering installing an illuminated mirror of the sort found in many a hotel room. They are quite expensive but they light up your face like nothing else and are the best by far for plucking eyebrows and seeing the bare-faced truth of your skin. There are a few dealers around. **Aslotel Ltd** (01372 362 533), for example, supply health farms and hotels with wall-mounted illuminated shaving mirrors. Revlon also do a free-standing version, available from branches of Boots.

☆

WHEN CLEANING MIRRORS, don't spray the cleaner directly onto the surface where it can drip into edges and damage the frame. Spray a glass cleaner onto a lint-free soft cloth and rub over the mirror. Then buff with a clean cloth to remove smears. Never use abrasive cleaners, which can scratch the surface.

TIPS ON ESSENTIAL OILS FOR THE BATHROOM

from Liz Earle

Essential oils contain volatile molecules which we inhale though the nose to directly affect the limbic system within the brain. Inhaling essential oils while sitting in a bath is the best way to benefit from their therapeutic qualities because the oils break down when they are burnt. Add them to a pre-run bath to prolong their potency, and buy organic oils where possible as they are likely to be of better quality. As a general rule, add five to ten drops to your bath.

Camomile is a wonderful oil to encourage a good night's sleep.

Ginger is warming and reviving, and is also thought to help combat colds and flu.

Jasmine is invigorating and helps to lift depression. It makes for a wonderfully luxurious bath.

Lavender can be used for a fortifying and calming evening bath.

Neroli is warming and relaxing and also helps to relieve anxiety.

The clean-up

GRIT YOUR TEETH and put on the Marigolds, as there is a price to pay for all that soporific soaking. Your bathroom is only going to be a gorgeous place to unwind if it is gleaming, but so long as it is cleaned regularly the bathroom should only take a minimal amount of time to deal with. Anyway, the shining chrome and porcelain surfaces that result should be enough to inspire you. If more incentive is needed consider this – ten minutes once or twice a week should be enough to maintain the room. Problems only really arise when the bathroom is left to fester and dirt builds up until it becomes hard to clear. First, if you have space, keep a bucket containing everything you need to clean the bathroom either in the room or somewhere near by. Then it's easy to whip around straight after a bath or shower when the surfaces are wet and warm and easier to clean.

Your cleaning kit should contain cloths for cleaning the sink, bath and any other surfaces, as well as a separate cloth to clean the loo. Washable cloths are better than sponges, which can hold bacteria. Soak the cloths each week in water and bleach to disinfect them, or use disposable ones. If possible, clean bathroom fixtures such as sinks and baths according to the manufacturer's recommendations. Some more abrasive cleaners should not be used on an acrylic bath, for example, though on an enamel bath it's perfectly safe. So what products you use depends on the surfaces that you have in your bathroom, but a basic kit should contain a non-abrasive cleaner such as a spray or liquid bathroom cleaner; a gentle abrasive such as Cif, and plain bleach. Rubber gloves are an essential, too, especially for the squeamish. And always rinse away all products thoroughly after use, then dry surfaces with a clean cloth to avoid limescale build-up.

○ DO avoid toxic commercial air fresheners and burn natural oils instead. Use an oil burner or put a drop of oil onto a lightbulb where the heat will disperse the aroma. Fresh white floral oils, such as jasmine and gardenia, are lovely for bathrooms.

○ DO use bleach with care as neat bleach will easily strip colour from carpet or any fabric it splashes on.

Cleaning surfaces

So long as they are dealt with often, cleaning porcelain or plastic sinks and baths should only take a few minutes. Specialist cleaners individually made for every conceivable job in the home are, in many cases, a marketing ploy, but in the bathroom the sort of dirt that accumulates is very different to that in the kitchen. Spray cleaners designed for the bathroom usually contain organic acids, such as citric acid, which will cut through the soap scum, while some also leave a glossy layer which prevents build-up and makes future cleaning easier.

New-generation cleaners require much less scrubbing too – in fact, they can usually be sprayed onto surfaces, left for a minute or two and then rinsed straight off, which is about as painless as cleaning gets. If possible, use spray cleaners close to ventilation to avoid inhaling fumes, and avoid aerosols, which will fill the atmosphere with toxins. However, with all the controversy surrounding modern cleaning sprays – which are thought to contribute to allergies and asthma – you might prefer to use more old-fashioned products, which also require some old-fashioned elbow grease, but are less likely to do you any harm. Or opt for 'green' products by producers such as Ecover, which do the environment less harm. These products are biodegradable, and packaged in recycled materials too.

Tiles and showers can be cleaned with the same bathroom sprays you use on baths and sinks, unless they are coated with a build-up of dirt. If so, then scrub them with a cream cleaner, such as Cif, which is more abrasive. Stainless-steel sinks need to be cleaned with a specialist product, or can be rubbed with baby oil and buffed to shine.

Limescale

In hard-water areas, limescale is unavoidable, and while there are perfectly good commercial limescale removers on the market, mineral deposits can be just as easily removed with distilled malt vinegar. Deposits usually coat shower doors and

☆

DO REPLACE WASHERS on dripping taps to minimize limescale and sink stains. If stains have already formed, scrub them with salt and distilled malt vinegar, then rinse.

tiles and build up around taps too. Other than drying off walls after every shower (which even the disciplined could find a bit too much of an effort), the best way to deal with limescale is to spray on a solution of vinegar and cold water and leave it to stand before scrubbing off the mineral deposits.

For taps and the surrounding area, soak some cotton wool pads or paper towels in a half-vinegar/half-water solution and drape it around the build-up. Leave overnight, by which time limescale should fall away quite easily. Soak showerheads in a vinegar solution and then remove further limescale with a piece of wire. To clean grouting, spray with a bathroom cleaner and leave it to stand for a few minutes or so, then scrub rigorously if necessary and rinse.

Mould and mildew

In a well-ventilated bathroom mould and mildew should be avoidable, but once they have taken root they are tricky to shift for good. While there are lots of specialist products to deal with the nasty black spots, a bleach solution will work just as well. Mix water and bleach together in a spray bottle, no stronger than one part bleach to four parts water, and spray the affected area. Over time, bleach can corrode grouting, so for really dirty patches you could also use a commercial grout cleaner from any big store such as B&Q.

Leave to stand for a few minutes then scrub away the mould and rinse the area well with fresh water before drying. To remove mildew from a shower curtain, wash in hot soapy water, rub with lemon juice and dry in the sun.

☆

DON'T LEAVE shower curtains bunched up after use – this is the quickest way to make them mouldy.

Loos

Loo cleaners often contain hydrochloric acid, phosphoric acid or citric acid, and are thickened to make them cling to the surfaces and hence clean more effectively. When you begin cleaning the bathroom, douse the inside of the loo with a specialist product or bleach so that it can get to work while you get on with the rest of the room. Bleach is certainly not a green product – the harsh chlorine solution of household bleach is one of the most toxic substances in the home, but it's essential for cleaning loos effectively. Wipe the outside of the bowl with a cloth soaked in a bleach solution, then scrub inside the loo with a brush, and flush. Wear rubber gloves and always use separate cloths to clean the loo (sponges are unhygienic), soaking them in a solution of bleach and water after use.

Plugholes and drains

It's easy to neglect pipes and drains until a problem occurs, which, in the worst case, could be a flood. When this has happened once it will make you a million times more vigilant. Drains need to be regularly maintained and you can begin by pouring boiling water down plugholes once in a while to clean any build-up of products. If water still doesn't drain quickly, then more radical steps are required. A natural alternative to using the commercial products available is to pour a cup of baking soda down the drain, followed by a cup of vinegar. Leave this for five minutes, then follow with a kettle of boiling water. Commercial products or caustic soda work in a similar way – they heat up and melt grease and dissolve any organic blockages such as hair, but they are highly toxic, so use with caution. Keep a window open for ventilation, always use rubber gloves and follow accompanying instructions with the greatest of care. It's a good idea to keep products like these in case of emergencies when less harsh solutions will not budge the blockage.

○ DO use boiling water to keep pipes and drains clear. Pour a kettle of boiling water down plugholes occasionally to sanitize and to clear any build-up of bath products – this is especially important for bath-oil junkies.

○ DO remove hair from plugholes before it can cause blockages, or buy a specially made mesh strainer.

○ DO make sure you always have the number of a plumber on hand in case of emergencies.

Heavenly sleep-inducing bath oils

REN's bath oils, packaged in clinical-looking glass bottles, have become something of a cult product. The oils disperse in the bath, softening the water without making it feel greasy. Moroccan Rose Otto is divine, although the High-altitude Lavender is the best for insomniacs. *(www.renskincare.com)*

Deep Relax Bath Oil by **Aromatherapy Associates** is probably the closest a product can get to a drug – the blend of camomile, sandalwood and vetiver is unbelievably pungent and within about ten minutes has the same effect as a wonderful relaxing massage. In the morning you smell delicious. If waking up is your problem then try their Revive oils, which are also very effective. *(www.aromatherapyassociates.com)*

Neal's Yard Remedies will blend bath oils to order – their website has a list of the properties of each essential oil, or you can consult staff at any of their stores. For a ready-made product, try their Soothing Bath Oil, which has calming geranium, lavender and cypress. *(www.nealsyardremedies.com)*

Laundry

Mastering washdays, from sorting and soaking to drying and pressing

IT'S UNDERSTANDABLE that laundry, more than any other chore, can induce feelings of domestic denial in even the most capable householder. Done without forethought, the washing, drying, ironing and folding of all your sheets, shirts and other clothing can seem like the greatest act of drudgery known to mankind, but there comes a point where we have to conquer our laundry phobia. There are two ways around this:

- Pay someone to come in and do it all for you, which is fine is you have the means.

- Or confront your fears, master the washday techniques and learn to love your laundry.

Focus on the good things about laundry: a pristine bed made with freshly laundered linens that have been line-dried in the summer sun and pressed with delicious-smelling lavender water, or a wardrobe filled with a supply of clean shirts that have been immaculately ironed.

Of course, our lack of enthusiasm for laundering might have something to do with our lack of knowledge when it comes to the ins and outs of washing, drying and ironing. If we knew exactly how to get a stubborn stain out of a white shirt, it would certainly make the job a lot more pleasurable. We all have traumatic memories of never-ending piles of ironing that have built up over months rather than weeks and make us dread ironing anything at all.

By learning how to get the best results and developing a common-sense routine, you'll find that the laundry will become a breeze. Dealt with regularly and efficiently, it will no longer sentence you to hours slaving with suds and steam iron. And by organizing the area in which washing, drying and ironing takes place, you make the task infinitely more enjoyable. Who doesn't dream of a fragrant utility room with neatly ordered shelves holding everything needed for wash-days, plus plenty of room for other household appliances to be conveniently stowed away?

Washing routines

First, you need to develop a routine that works for you – we all have different domestic patterns, but a methodical routine will save time and make the task much easier. Keeping up-to-date with laundry also prevents those depressing overflowing washing baskets, or dry and creased ironing that can seem overwhelming.

Get into the habit of stripping beds and replacing dirty towels on the same day each week, and, rather than leaving it until the weekend, do it on a Thursday or Friday so the week-end is kept wash-free. Get up an hour earlier one morning rather than trying to get it all done in the evening when you could be too tired. It seems so much more logical to get housework done at the end of the week. Who wants to spend all weekend toiling at home?

Sorting dirty laundry as you go will save time when it comes to washing. If you have space, then separate your wash-ing into different baskets, so that all whites are kept in one basket while colours are put in another, and so on. Multi-task where possible; while the washing machine is on the go you can whip through all the hand-washing and then dry it all at the same time. If you have somewhere to hang washing outside, make the most of sunny, breezy days when washing will dry quickly in the fresh air and have most of the creases blown out, which will mean little ironing or none at all, and deal with whatever needs to be pressed as promptly as possible – ironing fabrics straight from the washing line will be much easier than tackling a pile of washing with dried-in creases that prove virtually impossible to remove.

LAUNDRY ROOM ESSENTIALS

- detergents for machine and hand-washing
- soda crystals
- fabric softener
- pre-soak solution
- chlorine bleach
- plastic buckets for soaking
- household soap
- laundry basket
- pegs
- iron and ironing board
- clothes brush and pegs
- laundry rack
- lavender ironing water (not suitable for all irons)
- stain-removal kit
- sewing kit
- pilling machine or comb, and hooks to hang up other accessories such as mops and brooms

If clothes are cleaned straightaway you will also be able to get dressed much more quickly in the morning. A well-organized wardrobe where everything is always freshly cleaned and pressed is a joy, whereas on a rushed and stressful morning it is annoying and time-consuming to have to heat up the iron to press just one shirt.

Utility room/area

In an ideal world we would probably all like to have a capacious utility room with plenty of space for a washing machine and tumble-dryer, sinks for soaking and hand-washing and an old-fashioned drying rack. Custom-made shelving would house products and there would be room for all those other household appliances that are necessary but unsightly and hard to find homes for. The ironing board and iron could be stored away alongside brooms, mops and vacuum cleaner attachments, or stored flat on the wall where they will take up very little space.

But if you have a box room or large cupboard, you can come close to the ideal by maximizing space with a carefully thought-out plan. If there is space above the washing machine, make the most of the height of the room by building shelving on which you can stow all your laundry essentials, as well as some of those other housekeeping props. Another way to utilize the height of the space is to suspend a drying rack overhead that can be hoisted up out of the way; wet washing draped around the house is messy and depressing to look at. To make the most of a tight space, have hooks

UTILITY ROOM TIPS

from Cath Kidston

PAINT your laundry room in gloss white paint –
it always feels clean.

A SHELF around the top of the room, even if it is
hard to reach, is a great storage place and ideal
for vases.

AN AIRING CUPBOARD has to be warm. If it can't be
built in by your hot water tank, install a small
low-temperature heater in the cupboard.

OLD CHINA PLATES are great wall decoration in a
washroom instead of pictures, which can be
ruined by the humidity.

I ALWAYS KEEP A RADIO in the washroom and a stool
to perch on to do the ironing. If I had space,
I would fit in an armchair too and a pile of
books, as it is often the most peaceful place in
the house.

on the walls or the back of a door to hang up the ironing board, brushes and mops.

If the area you have for your washing machine and laundry accessories is more of a cubbyhole or simply a corner of the kitchen, fix a curtain across the front so you can hide everything away. Use a fresh ticking stripe or a gorgeous floral fabric that will inspire you to keep it all spick and span. Whatever the space you have for laundry, make sure that it is kept clean and tidy. Keep it well stocked so that all the products you need are always close to hand and you never find yourself without in an emergency.

○ DO use large jars to store products. If you don't like the ugly packaging of detergents, decant washing powder or tablets into a big glass jar with a screw-on lid.

○ DO keep the washing area well lit so you can see everything clearly. If possible, have a fold-down Formica work surface fitted that can be used for folding, stain removal or repairs.

○ DON'T store dirty washing in plastic bins – wicker or canvas laundry baskets are far preferable because they enable air to circulate around the laundry.

○ DO buy laundry products in bulk if you have ample storage space.

Detergents

Biological detergents contain enzymes that help to break down protein stains, making them effective even for fabrics that cannot be washed at a high temperature.

Non-biological detergents do not contain enzymes, which makes them more suitable for sensitive skin and for clothes that cannot be treated with biological detergents.

LAUNDRY HAMPERS

A WELL-THOUGHT-OUT box of laundry treats makes a perfect housewarming present for friends who are fond of all things domestic or for those who need some encouragement. Fill an old wicker basket or hamper with some lovely scented detergent and a linen spray such as L'Occitane's lavender water. You could also include old-fashioned wooden pegs, a pressing cloth and a few aromatic lavender bags (make you own with some pretty ticking or floral fabric if you have time). A scaled-down version of this would make a fun thank-you if you are staying with friends, while if you add beautiful antique linen to the basket you have created a very personal and unusual wedding present.

Gentle detergents (e.g. Woolite) are less alkaline than basic powders and liquids and so are essential for washing delicates and wool. (The alkalinity of most washing powders means they more easily remove grease and dirt but are harsher on your clothes in the process. Gentle detergents are less alkaline, sometimes to the point of being pH neutral.) Brands made specifically for wool are usually approved by the International Wool Secretariat and bear the Woolmark; they can double up and be used for silk and delicates as well.

Colour detergents (e.g. Persil Colour) do not contain optical brighteners or bleaching agents, which can change the colour of some fabrics.

Soda crystals (washing soda) were regularly used before high-tech detergents came on the market. They soften water, which facilitates cleaning, and also break down mineral deposits. A handful should be added to each wash in hard-water areas to prevent washing machines from becoming clogged up with limescale.

Pre-soak products (e.g. Biotex) contain enzymes that are effective in breaking down protein stains. They need heat to be effective, and items should be left in a pre-soak for at least an hour before washing. Stain sticks such as Vanish work in a similar way.

Fabric softener is used to soften fabrics and to reduce static electricity. Often heavily scented, it coats fabrics in a waxy film that also makes them less absorbent. It should be used sparingly or not at all on towels, sheets and T-shirts. Softening sheets for the tumble-dryer contain similar solutions in a dry form that is released in the heat of the dryer.

Bleach is a sanitizer and stain remover but can harm clothes, especially if it comes into contact with fabric without being diluted first. Buy unscented plain chlorine bleach for laundry and always dilute according to instructions before adding to the wash. Some fabrics should not be bleached at all – always check care labels. Sun is a natural bleaching agent and works brilliantly on white bedlinen and cottons.

Household soap is an old-fashioned product that is seldom seen these days but it is a very effective laundry aid. It should be worked into stains that have been dampened before adding garments to a machine-wash.

Designer detergents

Some of us need a little help with laundry motivation and the latest crop of stylish detergents and designer washday products certainly make the laundry a more tempting prospect. They cost much more than their commercial counterparts but the advantages are threefold. They smell divine – if you want to wake up to the waft of lavender or the heady scent of jasmine, these seductive soaps are for you. **Durance en Provence** detergents, softeners and laundry sprays are made with essential oils that lightly fragrance clothes and bedlinen (available by mail order: 01728 603310). The scent of lime blossom or orange flower is far preferable to the harsh chemical smell of big-brand detergents. Even if you can't afford to use such indulgent detergents regularly, they are lovely to keep for special occasions or to use as treats when you need cheering up or have guests coming to stay.

Designer detergents are usually packaged in gorgeous vintage-looking bottles with pretty labels or, in the case of some soap flakes, in kitsch tins that have obvious shelf appeal – they will transform your laundry area into a chichi washday haven.

Finally, and most importantly, the new generation of luxe-laundry products are often more environmentally friendly because in many cases they contain natural perfumes and biodegradable ingredients, as opposed to harsh chemicals that can be bad for your health as well as the environment. For everyday laundry they will clean just as well as harsher products and smell much more appealing.

Basic detergents

It's easy to be seduced by the seemingly endless array of new washing products on sale, promising everything from brighter whites to softer, fragrant laundry. There is no doubt that modern washing powders are more effective than ever – all those men in white coats are not toiling away for nothing – but it is more cost-effective to stick with the simplest detergent possible. High-tech powders that contain everything from bleaching agents to overpowering scents are, in reality, a false economy because they cannot be used for everything and could even damage your laundry if used for every type of wash. Strong-smelling detergents don't actually make clothes smell that great, they just give everything an overwhelming synthetic scent. Simply cleaned laundry smells the best, and if you want to add fragrance, add a few drops of essential lavender oil mixed with a few tablespoons of distilled malt vinegar to your softener compartment. Also try to avoid detergents with added softener, which affect the absorbency of your towels and bedlinen. If you want to use a fabric softener, buy it and use it separately, or, if you live in a hard-water area, add a small handful of soda crystals to the detergent to soften the water and reduce mineral build-up.

In most cases you will need only the most basic detergent – one for the machine and a gentle one for hand-washing delicates and wools. Some people also buy a detergent specifically for colours because they are free from the optical brighteners that over time can turn some fabrics dull or grey. Whether you choose to buy detergent in powder, liquid or tablet form is up to you – all will get the job done, but all have plus and minus points for you to weigh up. Traditional powders are by far the most economical, though they do take up more space and can be messy. Liquids take up less space and dissolve easily in cold water, which is useful for washing by hand. Tablets are space-saving but much more costly than a standard box of powder.

Always consult packaging for the correct dosage. If you use too little detergent, your laundry may not be cleaned thoroughly and may even end up looking grey, while too much powder might not be thoroughly rinsed away.

The right water

There's little you can do about the type of water you have at home but it's useful to be aware of how the type of water you have affects your washing, since the difference can be marked. In some towns or cities laundry never feels quite the same as a load washed in the countryside. This is one reason why Scottish cashmere is considered the best – throughout its manufacture it is repeatedly washed in pure Scottish water, which contributes to its softness. You will know if you have hard water – your kettle will get quickly coated in limescale, and the same stuff will coat the inside of your washing machine, too, making it less efficient over time as pipes become clogged up. Hard water also makes it difficult for detergent to dissolve efficiently, and can leave clothes hard too. As you can't change your water supply, it's worth adding soda crystals to each wash to soften the water and counteract the hardness. It will soften up your washing and over time will help to maintain the machine too.

Clothing care labels

While you are sorting a wash, consult the care labels to see what needs to be hand-washed or dry-cleaned and what can go in the machine. The fabric content generally indicates what type of care is required, but our clothes are becoming increasingly complex, with high-tech finishes and embellishments that can transform a simple T-shirt into a dry-clean-only top. Some clothes need to be dried flat, while others might need to be reshaped while damp. Even denim jeans these days can be deemed dry-clean only, so get to know your clothes and the special care they need. And always check labels before you buy clothes; regular dry-cleaning can cost a fortune.

While clothing care symbols are usually a good guide, it is also useful to learn when they can be ignored. More than ever before, manufacturers are bestowing dry-clean-only labels liberally in an attempt to cover themselves, escaping from any liability for clothes that are ruined in the wash. In fact, garments with a dry-clean-only label can often be hand-washed carefully. The best way to determine whether you can gamble is to think about the type of fabric the garment is made from – there is no reason why a plain silk top with no special finish or surface decoration cannot be hand-washed in cool water. But if a fabric has been treated with a special finish or is embellished with beading or embroideries, proceed with caution. If something is too precious to ruin, don't gamble by ignoring care instructions. Even pieces that could be safe to wash may need specialist pressing, so a professional dry-cleaner is often a safer bet. If you are in any doubt, always consult the designer or manufacturer of a garment so that it is on their heads if anything does go wrong and they are legally obliged to replace the item.

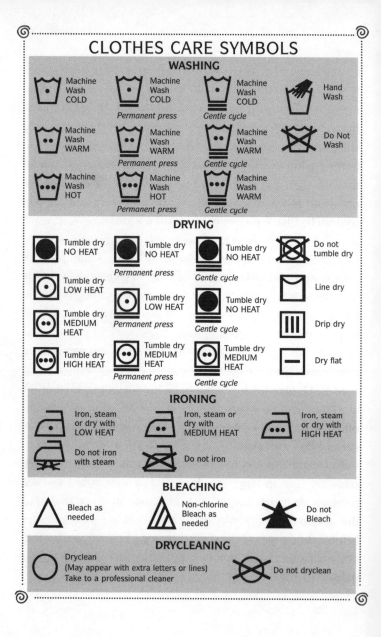

CLOTHES CARE SYMBOLS

WASHING

Machine Wash COLD

Machine Wash COLD
Permanent press

Machine Wash COLD
Gentle cycle

Hand Wash

Machine Wash WARM

Machine Wash WARM
Permanent press

Machine Wash WARM
Gentle cycle

Do Not Wash

Machine Wash HOT

Machine Wash HOT
Permanent press

Machine Wash WARM
Gentle cycle

DRYING

Tumble dry NO HEAT

Tumble dry NO HEAT
Permanent press

Tumble dry NO HEAT
Gentle cycle

Do not tumble dry

Tumble dry LOW HEAT

Tumble dry LOW HEAT
Permanent press

Tumble dry NO HEAT
Gentle cycle

Line dry

Tumble dry MEDIUM HEAT

Tumble dry MEDIUM HEAT
Permanent press

Tumble dry MEDIUM HEAT
Gentle cycle

Drip dry

Tumble dry HIGH HEAT

Dry flat

IRONING

Iron, steam or dry with LOW HEAT

Iron, steam or dry with MEDIUM HEAT

Iron, steam or dry with HIGH HEAT

Do not iron with steam

Do not iron

BLEACHING

Bleach as needed

Non-chlorine Bleach as needed

Do not Bleach

DRYCLEANING

Dryclean
(May appear with extra letters or lines)
Take to a professional cleaner

Do not dryclean

Washday

IF YOU HAVE DIFFERENT laundry baskets, much of the sorting will already be done. If not, separate washing first by colour, putting whites in one pile and colours in another. Then go through these piles sorting by type into hot washes or cooler ones, and put aside anything that needs to be hand-washed separately. Check every single pocket for anything you might have left there – an errant tissue can ruin an entire wash, while coins or metal can permanently damage the drum of your washing machine. Do up zips, hooks and anything else that could affect other laundry, and turn things that could fade inside out, such as denim, corduroy or sweatshirts. Put lingerie, lace or anything delicate that is going to be machine-washed into a specially made mesh washing bag or, if you don't have one, a pillowcase.

Next deal with stains. Remove any surface dirt or mud that could contaminate the rest of the wash by rubbing off any visible marks. Pre-soak anything with heavy stains that needs extra attention. To do this fill a plastic bucket with warm water and a pre-soak detergent and leave the item to stand for half an hour. Use soap to spot-treat stains and for perspiration marks and shirt collars: wet the soap, rub into the stained fabric and then allow it to work for a few minutes before adding the garment to the main wash. Then treat any other stain that needs specialist attention before washing (see pages 101–102).

Machine-washing

To get the most from machine-washed laundry, there are a number of things to consider. It is the combination of agitation, detergent and heat that will determine how clean your clothes get, so choose the correct cycle, temperature and products for the type of load you are washing and never overload the machine – the washing needs to have room to move or it will not get clean and the detergent will not dissolve completely. Overloading can also damage the machine.

○ DO wash heavily soiled things alone or pre-wash them separately by hand.

○ DON'T leave stained or heavily soiled laundry to sit for days on end or the stain will set.

○ DO carry out repairs before washing. If you wash anything that is ripped you could make it much worse.

○ DO try to wash sets of bedding or towels together so that they wear and fade equally over time.

○ DO wash new towels and sheets before use.

○ DO think twice before machine-washing blankets. They can shrink and also be tricky to dry thoroughly – it is better to have these professionally cleaned.

○ DO remove washing from the machine and dry it as soon as possible after the cycle has finished. Damp fabrics will start to smell if left for long periods and can also develop mildew.

○ DON'T spin-dry Lycra or stretch fabrics.

Washing machine care

To get washing really clean it is crucial to keep the washing machine running efficiently and to clean and maintain it regularly. Drawers, pipes and filters can easily get clogged up, which can prevent washing from being cleaned or rinsed properly or even cause permanent damage to the machine. First, make sure the machine stands on a sturdy, even surface; if allowed to move around, it could get damaged during a wash cycle. Regularly clean the soap drawer, which can become sludgy very quickly. Soak it in a bowl of hot water if necessary to remove any powder build-up. Each month empty the filter, which can get clogged up with debris from the wash, including fibres, limescale and any objects left in pockets by mistake. In hard-water areas washing machines can get particularly bunged up with nasty mineral deposits; to soften the water and so diminish limescale, either add a handful of soda crystals to each wash or once a month run the machine on the highest setting with soda crystals (or Calgon) in place of soap.

Do have your washing machine serviced. It is better to have it checked every other year than wait for it to get clogged up and, in the worst case, flood your home and cause irreparable damage.

Hand-washing

Cashmere, some silks, beaded fabrics and delicates all need to be gently washed by hand, as does anything else that is labelled for hand-washing. First, fill a completely clean sink with warm water, adding detergent under the running tap as you do so, and agitating the water until the detergent is totally dissolved. Never immerse items of clothing if there are granules of powder or clumps of liquid still visible. Wash each garment separately, starting with the lightest in colour, and gently squeeze the soapy water through the fabric, paying particular attention to any clearly dirty areas. Some hand-wash items can take more rigorous rubbing but this is not advisable for knits or delicates. After a few minutes, or when you think the item is clean, squeeze the excess water out and leave to one side. If colour has run, replace the soapy water with a fresh batch before washing the next thing. Once everything has been washed, you are ready to rinse. Again, immerse each piece separately (unless some are the same colour) and rinse each until the water is clear and all detergent has been removed. Squeeze out as much water as possible before drying; give sturdier things a short spin in the washing machine if necessary.

○ DO use a gentle hand-washing detergent for cashmere, wool and silk.

○ DO have a large clean surface where each piece of washing can sit before being rinsed.

○ DO beware of dark fibres getting attached to lighter fabrics and always wash lights and darks in separate water.

○ DON'T wring delicates or woollen clothes.

CASHMERE CARE

CASHMERE CAN BE HAND-WASHED, dry-cleaned or, for the brave, washed on a wool setting in the washing machine. The important thing is to stick to the same method of cleaning rather than chopping and changing. Some schools of thought advocate washing after each wear to keep the fibres flat, but you can prolong the wearing time of cashmere by wearing a vest or slip underneath the garment. If you wash at home, use a mild detergent (it should bear the Woolmark), but don't waste money on expensive specialist versions as gentle supermarket brands work equally well. Always wash very gently in cool water and never wring the knit. Don't use softener, which can 'felt' the cashmere and ruin it. Reshape the garment while it's damp and dry it flat on a plain towel. Store heavier cashmere over the summer months to protect it from moth attacks. Clean and dry thoroughly first, then wrap in acid-free tissue and store in boxes with cedar blocks or lavender.

TIPS ON DEALING WITH DELICATES

from Elspeth Gibson

Avoid CLEANING or washing heavily embellished pieces. They should simply be wiped down with a soft cloth and hung to air.

Very OFTEN intricate garments have removable linings that can be hand-washed and dry-cleaned. Some garments have detailed motifs that can be detached during dry-cleaning and then replaced.

Avoid IRONING or pressing your garment where possible. If you are going to hand-wash then take it to a professional to be pressed. If you feel confident, cover the sequins or beads with a clean tea towel; pressing through this will avoid melting the embellishment.

To FRESHEN VELVET and satin, hang and then steam the garment. Brush velvet with another piece of velvet to refresh the pile.

Look IN YOUR dry-cleaners or even your local superstore for the odourless mothballs you can now get, which can be stored in boxes or hung round hangers. They will protect clothes without making the garment smell fusty.

Stains

There are endless high-tech stain removers on the market (and time-proven tips that often work just as well) but first, before you panic and start to treat the stain, there are a few ground rules that apply to them all. Stains should always be dealt with as soon as possible before they have a chance to set. Begin by mopping up the excess, if necessary, working in towards the centre of the stain to keep it contained and avoid working the stain into the fabric. Never rub with a paper towel because this will make the mark even worse. Never apply heat to a stain; it is tempting to throw the item into the hottest wash possible but this could set the stain for ever.

Then consider what type of stain it is and what sort of fabric it is on. Protein stains such as blood, dairy products and egg need to be soaked in cold water with salt or with a biological pre-soak that will break them down. Similarly, if you are not able to treat a stain straightaway, then soak the item in a pre-wash and leave to soak until you are able to launder it properly. A pre-soak followed by a warm wash will remove most organic or food stains. For mineral deposits such as rust you should use an acid such as lemon juice or a commercial stain remover, which is based upon the same premise. Non-soluble stains, such as nail varnish, paint or glue, will need to be removed with a solvent and should always be treated separately before washing.

○ DO always test specialist stain removers on an inside seam before treating the stain.

○ DO try a solution of washing-up liquid, which will often remove stains caused by coffee, tea or fruit.

○ DO always rinse out the stain remover well before adding the item to a normal wash.

○ DON'T leave stains to set. Put them in a tub to soak if you don't have time to wash them immediately.

○ DO take dry-clean-only fabrics to be cleaned as soon as possible or the stain could become impossible to remove.

A to Z of stains

Chocolate Most chocolate stains will be removed quite easily in a normal wash cycle, but to remove any excess before washing, freeze the item and then scrape off while it is hard. If necessary, pre-soak, then wash as usual.

Coffee and tea Blot any excess, soak in cold water, work some diluted liquid washing detergent into the stain and then launder as usual. If the stain remains, or if it is an old stain, treat with a borax solution before re-washing.

Dairy products and egg Always treat with cold water. First, remove any excess, then soak in an enzyme pre-soak before washing according to care instructions. Borax can also be used effectively on protein stains before washing.

Fruit stains Remove any excess as soon as possible, then rinse with cold water. Work some diluted liquid washing detergent into the stain, then rinse with warm water. If the mark remains repeat the procedure. For a natural remedy, try using lemon juice or distilled malt vinegar on the stain: both of these remove most coloured food stains.

Grass Soak the fabric in an enzyme pre-soak or blot the stain with distilled malt vinegar before working detergent into the area, then wash as usual. Soaking in glycerine will also remove grass stains from white fabric.

Grease Treat make-up, oil, butter or mayonnaise stains with baking powder, which will absorb the stain. After removing any excess grease, rub the baking powder over the stain and leave it to sit for half an hour. Remove the excess powder before washing as usual.

Mud This should always be left to dry, then brushed off as far as possible. Launder in the cycle recommended for the fabric.

Nail varnish Remove any excess as quickly as possible, taking great care not to push the stain further into the fabric. After testing the fabric (such as on an inside seam), drip nail polish remover slowly over the stain while holding fabric taut. Repeat until the stain is removed and then wash as usual.

Pollen Use Sellotape to lift pollen from the fabric, then wash as usual. Some pollen (such as the rusty-coloured powder on lilies) will also need to be treated with a proprietary stain remover.

Red wine There are probably more remedies for the removal of red wine than anything else, from salt and soda water to splashing with white wine. How effective these are depends on the pungency of the wine and whatever it has been spilled on. Always soak up any excess as quickly as possible, then sprinkle with salt before rinsing with cold water or soda water, which should flush most of the stain away. Then wash as usual. If you are particularly prone to spilling red wine, invest in a specialist cleaner such as Lakeland's Wine Away, which works brilliantly on most fabrics.

Rust Stains can be caused by a rusty washing line or clothes pegs, but they can be removed with a commercial rust remover. For a natural remedy soak the fabric for half an hour in the juice of a lemon mixed with a tablespoon of salt before washing. Repeat if necessary.

Sweat Either soak with a pre-wash and then wash well, or for a natural solution soak in water with two tablespoons of white vinegar or lemon juice before washing as usual.

Tomato sauce and ketchup Remove excess before rinsing the stain in cold water. Soak in a pre-wash before washing.

Wax Scrape away any excess then lay the fabric over an old rag and cover with a piece of plain paper. Press down on the paper with a warm iron and the wax will gradually be absorbed. Repeat with clean paper until all of the wax has been absorbed then wash as usual.

Professional launderers

Having your laundry collected, then returned immaculately clean and beautifully pressed sounds like an indulgence that most of us can only dream of, but commercial laundering is much less expensive than it sounds. The royal launderer **Blossom and Browne's Sycamore** (020 8552 1231; *www.blossomandbrowne.com*), which is based in the East End of London, is one of the few remaining traditional launderers. It will collect and return free of charge in Greater London and also offers a postal service for anyone outside the capital. It will clean (and mend) virtually anything from City boys' shirts to bedlinen, duvets, pillows, eiderdowns and antique linens.

Sometimes it can be more economical to send laundry out; by the time you have washed and tumble-dried towels at home it can work out cheaper to have them professionally cleaned. Look locally to find a similar company close to where you live, and even if you can't afford to use them all the time they are a godsend over busy periods such as Christmas or holidays.

Drying and pressing

TO HELP CUT DOWN ON IRONING, try whenever possible to line-dry your washing outside. Wind will soften fabrics and knock out creases, and even in cities clothes and bedlinen will smell much fresher if they are dried outside rather than inside, especially on those bright, breezy days that are perfect for line-drying. The way in which clothes are hung will also make a big difference to how crease-free they become and how efficiently they dry.

Line-drying

First, always make sure the washing line is totally clean; any dirty marks will ruin all your clean washing and could stain light fabrics. Wipe the line with a wet soapy cloth, then run over it again with a clean cloth to remove any soap.

Before hanging anything give it a vigorous shake to get rid of any wrinkles and to restore the shape and, if possible, pull at side seams of garments, especially on jeans and trousers, to straighten them out. The way in which things are hung should not only retain their shape but also maximize the amount of air that can circulate around them. For larger items such as duvet covers and sheets, fold them horizontally, pinning them by the ends so as to create a loop through which air can blow. To retain the shape of shirts, either hang them on hangers or peg them by their tails to the line. T-shirts and tops should be pinned by the hem, but hang jeans and trousers by the waistband with the zip done up to help keep their shape. Skirts that are straight or A-line should also be hung by the waistband, though full gathered skirts can be hung by the hem so that air can circulate all around.

O DO always check that the washing line and pegs are totally clean and free from rusty patches that could inflict stains.

O DO hang white sheets in direct sunlight where they will benefit from the sun's natural bleaching. Equally, the sun can bleach colours and permanently ruin them, so try to hang these in shaded areas.

O DO dry heavy knits or beaded pieces flat rather than on the washing-line where they are liable to stretch out of shape.

O DON'T let laundry overdry or you will have a hard time ironing it.

O DON'T throw all your dry laundry into a basket. This will create more creases – fold things carefully, smoothing out any wrinkles.

O DON'T worry too much about laundry that has been caught in a rainstorm. The rainwater will provide an extra rinse for your washing and might even soften it up.

Drying inside

It is not always possible to dry clothes outside. If there are days of never-ending rain or you live in a town or city and have no garden or balcony, there is little alternative but to dry your laundry inside, unless you want to sit in your local launderette for hours. The same rules apply for clothes that are dried inside as for those hung outside. Give washed clothes a vigorous shake, and pull them back into shape by straightening hems and smoothing the fabric, before hanging them up on a rack or a clothes horse. Delicates and knitwear should be dried flat on towels positioned out of direct sunlight, but make sure that the towels are colourfast and will not stain the garments, and again pull the clothes back into shape before leaving them to dry. Don't dry laundry on or right next to a radiator; the heat can damage some fabrics.

Trouble-shooting

Colour runs happen to us all, though careful sorting should reduce the chances of it. If a load of whites has been coloured, the best course of action is to remove whatever caused the bleeding and wash the load again as soon as possible with Colour Run, which is sold in virtually all supermarkets. Alternatively, rewash the load with your usual detergent and a capful of chlorine bleach, which should return whites to their original colour. Unfortunately, there are some fabrics that will cling on to dye and cannot be whitened. Your only option is to dye them another darker shade or live with the new colour.

Faded fabrics that have been permanently lightened by the sun cannot be treated. The only course of action is to dye them a darker colour, if the fabric will take a dye. Never leave coloured clothes in direct sunlight for any length of time – some fabrics can fade within a matter of hours.

Pilling – the bobbling that occurs on fabrics, especially wool and cashmere – is caused by the friction that occurs during wear as well as washing. Washing wool after each wear is thought to prevent pilling, as it keeps the fibres flat so they are less likely to bobble. Wash woollen clothes inside out to reduce friction and also reduce the effect. See page 29 in the Wardrobes chapter for how to remove pilling.

Dry-cleaning

Complex fabrics, special finishes and overcautious manufacturers have all contributed to the increasingly common dry-clean-only label which, no matter how simple the garment, always sets off alarm bells in the domestically inexperienced. But even for those who know all there is to know about laundry it can still be a gamble to ignore the label and resort to hand-washing. Generally you should risk hand-washing only if you can cope with the loss of a beloved piece of clothing – if that beaded silk camisole is the most treasured thing in your wardrobe, it is always best to have it professionally cleaned. For more on hand-washing, see page 96.

For dry-cleaning, follow the rules listed overleaf so that you have to make fewer visits and so that you will know how to spot a good dry-cleaner that will take care of your clothes.

○ DO take stained clothes to the dry-cleaner promptly. Stains will be easier to remove the sooner they are treated.

○ DO always point out stains or marks to the dry-cleaner, even if they seem obvious … or embarrassing.

○ DO reduce dry-cleaning by brushing clothes after use and spot-cleaning them as well.

○ DO air-clean clothes if they come back smelling of the cleaning solvent – good dry-cleaners should, however, ensure that this doesn't happen.

○ DON'T keep clothes in the dry-cleaner's plastic covers; fabrics fresh from the cleaner's should be able to 'breathe'. If they must be covered, buy cotton garment bags for storage (see Wardrobes for stockists, page 22).

○ DO stick to the same cleaning process. If you dry-clean clothing once, then continue to do so, as this will help to stabilize the dyes.

Ironing

For many of us it is the most dreaded chore of all, but there are ways to make ironing more enjoyable and reduce the time spent doing it. First, by washing and drying things properly you will reduce the number of creases and in some cases might be able to do away with the iron altogether. To combat creases always dry following the procedures described on page 106 and always give laundry a vigorous shake before and after drying. Hanging shirts on hangers while damp encourages them to reshape themselves so that they need only a light press. Line-drying in a strong breeze can also help lessen creases and can sometimes smooth them out totally, but try not to let things become too dry or they will be impossible to iron. This is also common with hot tumble-dryers. If you overdry a load in a tumble-dryer, add a wet towel for a few minutes and the rest of the laundry will redampen. Once everything is dry, put away anything that doesn't need ironing: towels, some bedlinen, underwear, sweatshirts and most jeans will all be fine if they are neatly folded and left to air.

☆

CLEANING THE IRON

STEAM IRONS can quickly become clogged up with mineral deposits that will make them less effective and more likely to leave nasty marks on laundry.

To clean the iron mix a solution of distilled malt vinegar and water (1:4), pour it into the iron, turn it on and let it steam for five minutes before leaving it to cool. Then pour away the vinegar solution and rinse with fresh water. Do check that this is suitable for your iron, however – some self-cleaning irons should not be dealt with in this way. To clean the metal plate of the iron you will need to use a specialist iron-cleaning product.

If you are using a steam iron, make sure that the water level is topped up, then switch on and allow time for it to heat up. In the meantime, organize everything you need – set the ironing board at a comfortable height, and have a spray bottle of scented laundry water or plain water close to hand, as well as a pile of hangers and a clean surface for folding. Tune the radio to good ironing music (Radio 3 is especially good for ironing and not too distracting) and invest in a beautiful or quirky ironing-board cover to cheer you as you work.

Skilful ironing makes all the difference to how good your clothes look and how quickly you get the job done. An hour spent ironing is rewarding when everything ends up impressively pressed. When badly done, it seems hardly worth the effort. Take time to learn how to iron well and with practice you will cut down your ironing time. It's not just the heat of the iron that smoothes out creases but also the pressure, which is why it is crucial to have the ironing board at the right height for you, and why sitting down makes ironing harder work. If ironing is very creased douse it with a scented linen spray or plain water before beginning.

Start by ironing simple flat things, such as napkins and sheets. Smooth them across the board neatly, pulling them taut at the sides. Then, holding them flat with one hand, iron smoothly with the other hand. Fold large duvet covers in half and iron on both sides before turning back the other way and repeating.

Iron jeans and trousers without creases by flattening out each leg and pressing on both sides, smoothing out wrinkles as you go. Most trousers with creases will have to have them carefully ironed back in after washing.

Anything with a pile, such as corduroy, velvet and some heavy embroideries, needs special attention and preferably should be steamed rather than ironed. But at home corduroy and some velvets can be ironed lightly inside out with the pile side resting on a towel to prevent it from marking.

Delicates, silk and anything with surface decoration requires a pressing cloth, which can be any clean piece of fabric (even a tea towel). Iron the fabric inside out with the pressing cloth on top to protect it from the heat, and press the fabric lightly rather than moving the iron about too heavy-handedly. Most fabrics benefit from being ironed inside out as this prevents them becoming shiny from heat damage.

Anyone who understands how clothes are made is at an advantage when ironing, as the way in which seams, darts and pleats are pressed is crucial to how the finished item will look. The rule of thumb is to press clothes according to how they are constructed, which you can see by looking carefully – so iron over darts as they are sewn, iron seams inside out so that you follow the stitching, and iron in between gathers to retain the shape of the garment. Pleats, on the other hand, should be pressed with their sides pulled together because they should be flat when worn.

○ DO always test the heat of the iron first on something tough.

○ DO iron clothes according to care labels.

TIPS ON IRONING SHIRTS
from Sean O'Flynn, Shirtmaker at
New & Lingwood, Jermyn Street, London SW1

AFTER WASHING, give the shirt a good shake and then put it on a hanger so that it falls into shape as it dries – never leave it in a pile folded up.

When you are ready to iron, spray the shirt liberally with water and begin by ironing the collar on the wrong side from the outer corner in. Then repeat on the right side, pulling the corner up as you iron inwards – this will create a neat curve.

Now iron the yoke, first on the wrong side, then on the right side. Iron the cuffs, repeating the collar procedure and pulling the edge as you iron inwards.

Then tackle the back of the shirt on the wrong side. Next iron the sleeves, smoothing them on the ironing board as you go and paying careful attention to the gathers around the cuffs and the seams at the armholes. Sleeves can be ironed with or without creases (this is a matter of personal taste).

Finally iron the two front sections, moving around buttons and flattening out any creases around the armhole seams.

Leave to air on a hanger before returning to the wardrobe.

○ DO put a layer of aluminium foil underneath your ironing-board cover to reflect heat – it makes ironing much easier.

○ DON'T let a pile of ironing build up. By the time you tackle it, creases will be almost impossible to remove.

○ DO always iron linings before ironing the rest of the garment.

○ DO be careful not to pull too taut anything delicate or with a stretch, or you could distort the shape permanently.

○ DO air freshly ironed items on hangers or a clothes horse before storing away in case they are still slightly damp.

○ DON'T ever use a dirty or rusty iron.

Housework

*Cleaning routines and
how to keep house*

THE LIVING ROOM IS the most public area of a home and needs to look as neat and tidy as possible, but it's also the area that requires the lightest cleaning. Aside from an occasional thorough deep-clean, living rooms should be easy to maintain, unlike a bathroom or kitchen, which probably needs some kind of cleaning every day. A routine will make your life much easier. Spend some time once a week dusting, vacuuming and tidying up, and you'll only need a more thorough clean periodically. Learning how to clean effectively will cut down on the amount of work you have to do – there is, believe it or not, a right and wrong way to dust. Knowing how to look after your things will make it much less stressful to care for them. It's also worth remembering that the fewer possessions you have (and this includes everything from ornaments and knick-knacks to books and back issues of magazines), the less time it will take to clean.

Getting into a routine

Just the thought of a methodical routine or a cleaning schedule would make some people run for the hills, but the only sensible (not to mention simplified) way to deal with housework is to develop a plan that works with your lifestyle. If you prefer to dedicate your Saturday mornings to cleaning, you have probably already worked out a plan that is right for you. If your cleaning is more haphazard than that, then it's worth thinking about the way you organize your domestic life. If housework-free weekends sound appealing, if you like the idea that come Friday evening you can do whatever you want

without having to think about dusting away cobwebs or ironing a pile of shirts – try to get housework done during mid-
week mornings or evenings. The point of a routine is this:
when you do everything regularly and methodically, it not
only takes less time but also starts to fit neatly into your life.
In this way, you don't dread doing it, everything is always kept
up-to-date and in order. And when you can't keep up with
everything, learn to prioritize; the world will not come to an
end if you don't get round to vacuuming the carpets or dusting the living room.

○ DO have a major clearout to get rid of any
rubbish, and create proper storage areas for the
things you need to keep.

○ DO have a recycling box so that as soon as you
have finished with paper and magazines, they can
be put away.

○ DO keep ornaments to a minimum. They can
provide convenient cover for piles of dust. Where
possible, avoid open shelving, which will encourage a build-up of dust and dirt.

The spring clean

To the uninitiated, spring cleaning sounds deceptively appealing, but anyone with wistful images of Doris Day waltzing
around in a headscarf and gingham apron should think again

– spring cleaning requires a lot of organization and hard work. However, all the toil and sweat is well worth it; there's nothing like having a total clearout and cleaning your home from top to bottom before the long, light days of summer.

There's no particular reason why a thorough clean should be done in the spring. It was traditionally done at this time of year after long winters during which wood or coal fires made houses filthy with soot. Our homes are now much cleaner year round, and doing a big clean in the spring isn't essential. However, there is a seasonal logic to it, although cleaning in the autumn definitely has the same kind of therapeutic benefit. Try to clean on a bright, breezy day when you can have the windows thrown open for ventilation and can see more clearly all the benefits of your hard work.

Spring cleaning used to involve tackling the entire house from top to bottom, but this is a task only for cleaning extremists. Instead, focus on one or two rooms, and ideally try to dedicate a whole day or a weekend so you can get the job completely finished. Once you have decided when you are going to begin cleaning, you need to get organized. The first thing to do is to make a list of everything that needs to be done arranged in a logical order. This means cleaning from the top to the bottom of each room, and going from wet to dry. Also consider doing the toughest jobs first, or the ones you are dreading most, so you get them out of the way early on. Then you are less likely to feel like giving up when you are halfway through.

Make sure you have everything you need to get it all done in one go (see Spring Cleaning Kit on page 124). And never try

SPRING CLEANING TIPS

THIS IS A GOOD opportunity to have soft furnishings, curtains or bedding that cannot be washed at home professionally cleaned. Do this before you start so that they will be ready when you have finished.

START AT THE TOP of the room and remove light fixtures that need to be cleaned. Shades might only need to be dusted well or lightly wiped with a damp cloth, while chandeliers require a more thorough clean (see page 135).

IF YOU NEED TO wash down walls, cover furniture with sheets to protect them from splashes. To wash painted ceilings and walls from top to bottom, use a sugar soap solution from a DIY shop. This strips away dirt, but as it's powerful it can also leave streaks so clean the entire area methodically and thoroughly.

CLEAN UNDERNEATH all furniture as well as skirting boards and concealed areas, which are a mecca for dust and dirt.

SILVER CAN ALSO be washed in a mild detergent, but tarnishing needs to be treated with a special polishing cloth. Once the tarnish has been fully removed, buff with a dry cloth until the silver is gleaming.

GENTLY WASH china ornaments by hand with warm, soapy water and a soft cloth, then rinse and allow to dry. Some china can be put into the dishwasher, but never take risks with precious antique pieces.

HIRE A CARPET CLEANER and shampoo carpets if they look like they need it. A thoroughly cleaned carpet looks almost as good as new.

AREAS THAT ARE frequently touched accumulate dirt. Wipe down light switches, door handles, banisters and other obvious areas with a well-wrung soapy cloth. Baby wipes, if you have some of them to hand, are a useful quick-fix cleaner.

USE THE VACUUM-CLEANER attachments to suck up cobwebs from ceilings, walls and cornices, or use a long-handled feather duster.

SHUTTERS AND BLINDS need to be dusted and washed. If they are very dusty and can easily be taken down, then take them outside and shake away most of the dirt first. Then brush if necessary before washing them thoroughly.

CHECK AND REPLACE smoke-detector batteries.

DON'T WEAR ANYTHING precious when cleaning. Jewellery can get scratched or tarnished and clothes can get stained by cleaning agents.

THE RIGHT MUSIC is a cleaning tool just as important as all the rest! It will distract you from the amount of hard work you are doing. Music for cleaning needs to be upbeat to keep you moving, and if it makes you sing along, even better.

to clean a cluttered room. The mess will make the job twice as hard. Have a major detox first, throwing away anything that can be disposed of (such as old magazines, papers and other clutter using up precious space) and storing other things that could get in the way of your clean-up. Don't forget to empty cupboards and shelves.

Hiring a cleaner

It might sound like a huge indulgence but if you really hate cleaning (or specific bits of it), then hiring some part-time help could make a huge difference to your quality of life. It's not just big households that hire cleaners these days. As time seems to be the commodity in shortest supply, people from single girls with busy careers to time-pressed mothers are paying someone to do the chores they don't have the time or inclination for.

The best way to find a cleaner is by word of mouth. Do you have friends who live close by who could share their (tried, tested and super-reliable) cleaner with you? Alternatively, ask around locally or place ads in small shops or newspapers to find someone who lives nearby. When you find someone, interview them and try to ascertain if they share your standards, which should ensure that they do as good a job as you could hope for. If they give written references, always chase these up on the phone, asking as many questions as you can think of. Remember that you will be handing over the keys and security of your home to this person, so you need to feel totally at ease with them.

When you have found someone you trust, make a list of exactly what you would like them to do – you have hired a cleaner, not a psychic, remember. Make sure you provide them with everything they need to do the job, and if there are products they prefer to use then consider buying these too. As clutter will simply slow them down, tidy up a little before they arrive to make their job easier. If you want them to do more than light cleaning, you should allow them plenty of time. Don't expect a cleaner to do anything in less time than you could feasibly do it.

Rates vary widely, depending on where you live. You could call local cleaning agencies to get a rough idea – although their rates will usually be about 25 per cent or more than the cost of hiring someone privately.

○ DO let your cleaner know if there is something you are not happy with – be straightforward and up front, and deal with the problem straight away. While you want to keep your cleaner happy, you shouldn't be terrified of letting them know how you prefer things to be done.

○ DON'T expect them to do any more than you would: they can't spring clean in a day. If you want extra work done, be prepared to pay for it.

○ DO give them breathing space if you work from home. No one will want to work for you if you follow them round inspecting and taking notes.

○ DO treat your cleaner with care. Leave treats,
work on developing a good relationship and if
you can pay them over the odds, do so – you will
probably get better service.

○ DO warn them about anything precious: antique
glasses that can't go into the dishwasher, delicate
antique rugs that can't be hoovered, French
polished tables that mustn't get damp, etc.

Cleaning kit

Domestic chores will be much easier and more enjoyable if
you have a neatly ordered cupboard with everything you need
close at hand. It will also make you feel organized and quite
saintly even before you tackle a single thing. Make sure that
the cupboard is well stocked before you begin any kind of
major cleaning.

It's impossible to ignore the increasing evidence that
some household cleaning products can do us physical harm.
There are toxins in everything, from some paints and carpets
to powerful detergents, and they have been linked with ill-
nesses from asthma to various types of cancer. Many of us
would be loath to give up the modern cleaning products that
make our lives a whole lot easier, but it is prudent to use them
as little as possible. Always follow instructions and make sure
that rooms in which they are used are well ventilated so toxins have a way out. Aerosols are among the worst offenders
because they fill a room with fine airborne chemicals for us to

CLEANING KIT

- heavy dusters
- cloths that can be laundered
- broom, dustpan and brush
- vaccum cleaner and bags
- all-purpose spray detergent
- bleach
- window cleaner or distilled malt vinegar
- specialist polishes (ie. for leather)
- cleaner for wooden furniture or antiques

inhale, so use pump-action spray cleaners instead, which only go where you point them, or, better still, cleaners that are poured from the bottle. Never mix up different products in a bid to create a super-powerful cleaning agent, and never ever mix chlorine bleach with any other cleaning product – this can produce highly toxic chlorine gases.

Wood and laminate floors

Wooden floors are blissfully easy to clean but they are totally unforgiving when it comes to showing the dust and dirt. If you have many wooden-floored rooms it could be worth investing in a dust mop; otherwise begin by gently running the vacuum cleaner over the boards, which will remove most of the dust. Always clean along the length of the boards, and use the appropriate attachment to clean around edges and along skirting boards. If marks remain, you may need to go over the floor with a well-wrung mop or sponge. Using a mild detergent, wash the boards carefully, then go over them again with a rinsed, well-wrung cloth before leaving to dry. This is the best method for cleaning laminate floors, too, although waxed wood should never be washed. If stubborn marks still remain, spot-clean them with a soapy cloth or, if necessary, remove with a dab of white spirit.

While few of the aggressively marketed 'super products' around these days are worth the extra money, the long-handled floor cleaners created to clean wooden and laminate flooring are worth investing in. They work with a disposable cloth that clips on and magically picks up all the dust, hairs and other bits of dirt from the floor – they make floor-cleaning utterly painless and are also great for a quick cosmetic clean when you don't have the time or inclination for the whole works.

○ DO use coasters under the feet of furniture to protect wooden floors and carpets.

○ DO clean up spills straight away as liquids damage wood quite quickly.

○ DON'T drag furniture over wooden boards: it might scratch and dent them. Always lift furniture from one place to another.

○ DON'T walk around in spike-heeled shoes – when it comes to wooden floors, they are the enemy.

Carpets and rugs

The simplest way to keep carpets and rugs looking good is to prevent them getting too dirty in the first place, so use door mats both inside and outside. Don't wear outdoor shoes around your home. If you feel awkward asking guests to remove theirs, leave a line of brightly coloured leather or suede Moroccan slippers by the door to make it more enticing.

To keep carpets looking good, thoroughly vacuum them at least once a week to pick up dust and dirt. When doing a bigger clean, take rugs outside and give them a good beating, leaving them to air if possible. Always deal with spills or dirty marks as soon as they happen to stop any stains settling in. Mop up the excess first, blotting liquids with kitchen paper and working inwards from the outside of the spillage. Never rub or you will force the stain further into the carpet. If possible, put kitchen paper underneath to absorb any liquids that soak through. Then use carpet shampoo to thoroughly clean the area, following the manufacturer's instructions, and rinsing with fresh water. If the area is lighter when dry, you may have to shampoo the whole carpet so it is uniformly clean.

○ DO empty vacuum cleaner bags regularly. Change them in a well-ventilated spot, preferably outside.

○ DO think about investing in a steam-cleaner, which cleans carpets, rugs and natural flooring thoroughly and without the use of toxic chemicals.

HOME FRAGRANCING TIPS

from Jo Malone

FILL DRAWSTRING BAGS with fresh lavender, rosemary and tiny eucalyptus leaves and place them behind cushions on the sofa. As soon as someone takes a seat, the bag is crushed and releases the fragrance.

PLACE BOWLS of fresh herbs around the house before going on holiday to keep rooms fresh for your return. Eucalyptus bunches are great for this as they dry naturally and have a very clean scent. (Bunches of herbs can also be used as decorations for the Christmas tree. They look and smell divine.)

FOR DINNER PARTIES, spray tablecloths and napkins with Acqua di Limone linen spray – as guests unfurl their napkins a very subtle scent of lime water is released. After dinner, light grapefruit-scented candles to clear and freshen the air.

SPRAY FRESHLY LAUNDERED linens with Lino Nel Vento linen spray to lightly scent with lavender, or when you have friends or family to stay, spritz just under the pillow before bedtime and allow the scent to settle. There's nothing more comforting than climbing into crisp white linens with the subtle fragrance of the Mediterranean to encourage sleep.

○ DO treat indentations on wool carpets with an
ice cube. Let it melt and the wool will rise up again.

Dusting

There's more to dusting than prancing around with a few
ostrich feathers or a felt cloth. The quickest way to master the
art is to understand the way in which the dust builds up. Dust
moves stealthily from place to place on air currents, which is
why no matter how often we clean it still reappears in no time
at all. The more we move around, the more the dust moves
too, but by reducing the places in which it can run and hide
(which are usually the nooks and crannies you don't bother to
dust when cleaning), the amount of dust can be dramatically
reduced. Clutter will provide plenty of hiding places for dust
– neat, sealed storage will help to minimize this.

First, as with any cleaning, always dust from top to bottom, beginning with light fixtures, cornicing, ceilings and
walls, removing dirt and cobwebs with a long-handled feather
duster. The old-fashioned ostrich dusters are the most effective. They lift off dirt and cling on to it without depositing it
elsewhere (and those beautiful soft brown feathers look lovely
too), but the lamb's wool versions are also very good. Don't
just whisk it through the air, redistributing the dust; when you
think you have picked up lots of dirt and dust, take the duster
outside and give it a good shake.

On areas lower down, use a heavy soft cloth that will pick
up dust effectively. Wherever possible move pieces of furniture because dust tends to pile up in hidden areas: alongside

concealed skirting boards and around the backs of chairs and so on. Wipe over the feet and legs of tables and chairs you might normally forget. Equipment such as televisions and stereos attract dust with their static electricity so these will need to be carefully and thoroughly wiped down with a clean cloth – do it slowly so as not to flick the dust elsewhere.

Books attract a lot of dust, especially if they sit unused for a long time, so run a feather duster over the tops of these, or go over them gently with the upholstery attachment of your vacuum cleaner, or use a library brush. When you have finished dusting, tap your feather duster outside to lift off excess dirt and put dirty cloths through the wash.

Cleaning wooden furniture

Old wooden furniture needs to be cared for correctly if you want to maintain the patina that has built up over time. Avoid using spray polishes, which, with repeated use, will form an unwanted coating on furniture. Instead, treat wood a few times each year with a beeswax polish, which should be rubbed into the surface and then buffed with a clean soft cloth. Between treatments, dust furniture regularly with soft dusters to maintain a shine. If you do want to use a spray polish, always apply it to the cloth and not straight onto the piece of furniture, and buff well to remove as much of the polish as possible. If you need to remove sticky marks, use a very well-wrung soapy cloth and then rub over with a rinsed cloth before drying.

◯ DO treat white rings left from cups or glasses
with a little beeswax, but only when they are totally
dry. Alternatively, try rubbing with a tiny amount
of Brasso.

◯ DO keep furniture away from direct sources of
heat and light.

◯ DO always check how to clean valuable furniture
when you buy it, or consult the **Association of
Art and Antique Dealers** (020 7823 3511 or
www.lapada.co.uk) for advice on cleaning or
finding a restorer to treat damaged pieces.

Soft furnishings

When you buy any soft furnishings, from curtains to chair
covers, always check the laundering instructions. Washable
upholstery can safely go through the washing machine, but do
make sure you will be able to get it totally dry too, and expect
a little shrinkage when washing for the first time. Other soft
furnishings, especially anything in velvet, silk or even heavier
cottons, will be 'dry-clean only', in which case don't even consider washing them yourself. Take them to a dry-cleaner. It
will be expensive but preferable to squeezing your three-seat
sofa into a cover that's shrunk to fit a two-seater.

It's nice to trade heavier curtains for lighter ones in the
bedroom in the summer. Lightweight summer curtains can
usually go in the washing machine (again, check washing

FLOWER TIPS

from Ercole Marconi of McQueen's

ALWAYS PUT FRESH FLOWERS into clean water as soon as possible after buying them. Take about an inch off each stem at a 45-degree angle – cutting them under running water will prevent air getting into the stem and the water will get in more quickly.

WOODY-STEMMED flowers will absorb slightly warm water more quickly.

REMOVE ANY LEAVES from the part of the stem that will be submerged because they will rot and pollute the water.

IF YOU DON'T HAVE flower food, add a little sugar to the water along with a teaspoon of bleach. This will make your flowers last longer – the glucose in the sugar provides food for the flowers while the bleach kills bacteria.

KEEP FLOWERS OUT of direct sunlight or the heat from fires or radiators. Drafts and air-conditioning will make the flowers die more quickly. Some fruits (bananas in particular) can also have an adverse effect on flowers, so keep flowers away from fruit bowls too.

TO REVIVE DROPPING tulips, wrap the heads in paper for an hour, then cut the bottoms and arrange them.

instructions first). Keep curtains you need to have professionally laundered as dust-free as possible by taking off superficial dirt every so often with the soft upholstery attachment of your vacuum cleaner. And always line good curtains with equally good lining. If you spend a fortune on beautiful curtains and don't protect them properly, the sunlight will rot them over time.

○ DO use throws to protect furniture. They can be washed easily and are a useful alternative to loose covers.

○ DO put washable net curtains through the washing machine with a little bleach if they are really grubby. Put them into a mesh bag first if they are delicate.

○ DO put cushion and sofa covers back on when they are still very slightly damp to counteract any shrinkage.

○ DO keep precious soft furnishings (and furniture for that matter) out of direct sunlight, which can fade and eventually rot many natural fabrics.

Sparkling windows

It's quite easy to ignore how dirty your windows are (especially if you can hide them behind net curtains) until you've seen the home-enhancing effect of a gleamingly clean pane of glass. Sparkling clean windows make a huge difference to how your house looks, both inside and out. The easiest option, of course, is to pay someone else to do it, especially on the outside. If you have big sash windows or ones that are difficult to reach, then the cost will be worth every single penny. Finding a good window cleaner, or any window cleaner at all, is easier said than done, however, especially in big cities, but asking neighbours (with sparkling windows) who they use or stalking your local streets during the day are good ways to find someone local and reliable.

If you are tackling the windows yourself, here's how to do it. Clean the frames first with a soapy wet cloth (washing-up liquid is fine for this) until all the dirt is removed. If this hasn't been done for a long time, it may take a few washes to get the wood totally clean. Then wipe the frames clean with a damp cloth.

If you are using a commercial cleaner such as Windowlene on the glass, then follow the instructions on the bottle, which usually involves rubbing a small amount of the product in and then wiping it away with a clean cloth and buffing well to remove all smears. Always use non-linting cloths or you will end up with lots of nasty filaments, which are tricky to remove. Alternatively, you could use a solution of water and ammonia or distilled malt vinegar, which cleans equally well. Wash down a couple of panes of glass at a time, then gently sweep away liquid with a squeegee. You will need to wipe the water from the squeegee often or you will end up sloshing water all over the clean bits. Use a soft dry cloth to wipe away any moisture or smears.

Lampshades and chandeliers

Light fittings and chandeliers gather an incredible amount of dirt and dust, especially if you only get round to cleaning them as part of an annual clean. Remove surface dust on lampshades with a soft brush and follow by wiping with a soapy cloth. Be sure to wipe around light bulbs, too, which tend to gather a lot of dust – remove them from the light fitting before you do this.

Chandeliers require more thorough and careful cleaning. If they can easily be moved, then take the whole chandelier down. Remove all the crystals and wash them in warm soapy water before rinsing and drying on clean tea towels. Wash the frame of the chandelier with a soapy cloth, then wipe over with a clean cloth before leaving to dry.

Some chandeliers will have to be cleaned while they are hanging. Put newspaper or a waterproof sheet on the floor underneath to catch any drips. Fill a bowl with warm water and some washing-up liquid and gently wash down with a soft cloth. Allow to drip-dry. A solution of vinegar and water also works well on chandelier crystals. For ones that are covered in nicotine, use Antiquax's chandelier cleaner, which you can buy from lighting specialists – this can be sprayed onto the crystals and it will drip off, taking all the dirt with it.

Making a real fire

Real fires make any room instantly cosy and comforting. First, if you have not lit a fire before, ensure it is safe to do so. Have chimneys swept every few years or you could get smoked out or, much worse, if there are any blockages in the chimney, a fire of the entirely wrong sort could start. Clean out the grate to remove all the old ash and begin with a totally clear area so that air can circulate around the fire. Begin by making a neat pile of tightly screwed-up newspaper in twists or balls in the centre of the grate, then arrange pieces of dry kindling (the small bits of wood that will get the blaze going quickly) all

around this pile. Light the newspaper and allow the flames to become established before adding small logs or pieces of coal to the top of the fire using fire tongs. As the fire becomes established, add larger logs until the blaze is well and truly going. Use a guard to stop embers flying from the grate.

Household pests

Ants While they do not pose any kind of hygiene threat, ants can be a pain, especially when they are marching arrogantly across kitchen surfaces in a military formation. The only way

CANDLE TIPS

from Laurent Delafon of Diptyque UK

NO MATTER HOW SAFE you think they are, candles should never be left unattended. Always burn them on a solid, heatproof surface.

ALWAYS TRIM the wick after use to 1cm, or 1.5cm maximum. This prevents the candle from 'smoking' and also allows the candle to burn for longer.

ALWAYS RECENTRE the wick when you blow out the candle to ensure it burns evenly next time.

NEVER PLACE candles in a draft where they will burn quickly.

BURN YOUR CANDLE for one or two hours at a time – after this time the scent should fill the room.

TO COUNTERACT cigarette and cigar smells, use spicy scented candles (Diptyque's *Thé*, *Pomander*, *Opopanax* and *Oranger* are all good examples).

to eradicate them is to locate their nest by tracking their movements and then – and this is not the best approach for animal-lovers – either pour boiling water into it or douse with an ant powder. If you cannot find the nest, spray powder around window and door frames and any other areas where they could enter. In the kitchen, keep cupboards and surfaces scrupulously clean to discourage ants from moving in.

Flies These are unavoidable household pests, especially over the summer months when they are more numerous and can easily fly in through open windows and doors. Flies carry nasty germs so keep food well covered or stored in tightly sealed containers, wash down kitchen surfaces often, and avoid leaving sinkfuls of washing-up for any length of time. Use fly spray to kill them, or better, since these kinds of spray are incredibly toxic, use more environmentally friendly methods. Flies dislike strongly scented oils such as lavender or eucalyptus, so heat essential oils in a burner or leave bunches of the herb by doorways and windows.

Cockroaches They love moist, warm areas and tend to huddle around dark, damp corners of the kitchen. They can carry disease and contaminate food so it's important to deal with them quickly. As they are incredibly resilient, it's usually best to seek a local pest-control company (see page 140) if you are overrun with the nasty creatures.

Fleas If you find you are getting bitten or happen to see a flea hopping around, your home could be infested. If you have pets, treat them with the appropriate spray, make them wear flea collars and wash their bedding regularly on a high setting. In the home, vacuum the infected areas thoroughly (and then empty the vacuum cleaner bags) and wash soft furnishings. Then treat the area with an over-the-counter insecticide. If outbreaks are more serious, you may have to call in experts for thorough fumigation. Fleas are at their peak throughout August and September, and often break out when we leave homes empty. With no vacuum-cleaning being done, they happily multiply. However, with Cat in the cattery, they have nothing on which to feed. (While they were munching on Cat, you probably had no idea of their existence.) So you return after your summer holiday to a house full of hopping mad, hungry fleas. It's not only pet owners who have flea problems, either; anyone can carry fleas into their home, and flea pupae can lie dormant for up to a year. If you move into a new property, for example, you could find yourself with an infestation.

Mice Small rodents can carry diseases into your home, contaminate food and cause damage with their gnawing. Prevent them from getting in by sealing up any gaps or openings, although mice can squeeze through the tiniest spaces. Discourage mice by keeping food stored correctly, by keeping cupboards, larders and surfaces really clean and by emptying and cleaning dustbins as regularly as possible. If you have the stomach for it, you can capture the rodents with commercial traps, but otherwise call in professional pest control.

Silverfish Often found in dark moist areas, silverfish will munch through wallpaper, books and some fabrics. To avoid infestation, keep areas as clean as possible. If necessary, use insecticide around where they have been spotted. Starched fabrics such as linen left in storage for long periods of time will often have yellow stains caused by silverfish.

Wasps It is advisable to leave wasp and bee nests unless they pose an obvious threat. If you are determined to deal with a wasp nest it is better to call in professional help – while it is possible to deal with them yourself, you may not be up to batting a swarm of enraged stinging insects. Bees are a protected species and must not be destroyed. If you cannot live with them, your best option is to find a local beekeeper who will safely move the swarm away.

Foxes These are increasingly common in urban areas, making their homes under shrubs and in cosy garden corners. While they are unlikely to cause any harm (unless you have a cute bunny rabbit in the garden), they can be noisy, leave strong scents and rummage through rubbish. Block holes in fences to discourage them coming in and, if you have a serious fox problem, call the **RSPCA** (0870 5555 999; *www.rspca.org.uk*).

To locate **pest control** in your area, call your local council or contact the **British Pest Control Association** (01332 294288; *www.bpca.org.uk*)

The Kitchen

*Buying the right kit and
how to look after it*

KITCHENS HAVE BECOME so much more than functional spaces where we simply get something to eat – they can be the hub of the home where we entertain friends with cosy suppers or where we indulge in a Saturday afternoon baking. The kitchen also needs a lot more care than most other rooms in your home. It needs some degree of cleaning every day, and the cleaning needs to be thorough and methodical. A kitchen is worth investing in: it gets daily use so it deserves as much planning, equipping and maintenance as you can lavish on it.

Order is also key. You should be able to locate your utensils without rummaging through cluttered drawers, and reach for the lemon juicer without having to remove the entire contents of a cupboard. The best way to keep the kitchen streamlined is to stock it wisely with truly useful things that you need and do actually use. The choice of kitchen equipment is confusingly extensive. Do you need those very expensive but rather gorgeous-looking gleaming knives, or will cheaper ones work just as well? The answer is to spend as much money as you can on key pieces. Start with the crucial things, gradually building a collection with everything you need.

Cleaning the Kitchen

Get into the habit of cleaning everything as you go along so that surfaces are always clear and wiped down. Try to wash up regularly, and especially last thing at night, so that plates and pans are never left to fester. Always wipe down surrounding surfaces too. It takes discipline but most kitchen cleaning can be done quickly if you keep up-to-date. Then, once a week or fortnight, clean more thoroughly: disinfect bins, clean the fridge, wash the floor and so on. Major tasks such as cleaning cupboards can be done as part of a seasonal spring clean, although if everything is stored well and you clean up spillages whenever they occur, cupboards should stay pretty pristine.

Arrange your kitchen so that things are exactly where you need them. It sounds obvious but it needs to be given a bit of thought to get right. Think about how you cook and then arrange utensils so that they are always at hand – it will make cooking much easier. And remember when planning your storage that while open shelving can be convenient (as well as a good way to display all your shiny pans and gadgets), everything will get dusty. It works in a professional kitchen because most things are used every day, but at home it is better to have on display only the things that you regularly use.

The washing-up

For something so simple, it is staggering that so many people are clueless when it comes to the washing-up. If done correctly (so that everything gleams), washing-up should not take too long and should be a pretty painless chore. First, try to wash dishes promptly – the longer they are left, the harder they are to clean, and it's also disheartening to have to look at a sinkful of dirty dishes every day, not to mention smelly, too. Piping-hot soapy water is essential to get everything clean, and it should be changed often if you have a vast pile of washing-up to do. Wear rubber gloves if the heat is too much, but don't wash delicate glasses wearing gloves or you are likely to drop them and smash them.

Arrange all the washing-up in order. If you have heavily soiled dishes, put them to soak in warm soapy water while you are washing everything else. Clear as much debris as possible. Pour cooking fats into a plastic tub rather than down the sink where they can cause blockages. If there is a lot of washing-up to do, you can also rinse everything first under a hot tap to make washing-up easier. Stick to a logical order and wash like with like to make the process quicker. The least dirty things should be cleaned first: this usually means glasses, then move on to crockery, cutlery, serving dishes and finally saucepans or baking dishes. Once clean, rinse each piece to remove any soapy residue as you go – this is crucial for smear-free glasses.

There are different schools of thought over whether it is best to air-dry or hand-dry dishes. If you air-dry, everything will dry more quickly if it is first rinsed in piping-hot water. Once dry it should be put away rather than left to stand. If you dry by hand, always use a clean tea towel, so as not to contaminate clean dishes, and use non-linting towels to get glasses clean and sparkling.

Clean the sink after washing up, too. Occasionally you can use a bleach solution, if it needs it, and also pour a kettleful of boiling water down the plughole to clean drains and prevent any blockages. Finally wipe down surrounding areas with a general cleaner and wipe dry. Traditional dishcloths are the best things to use for washing-up because they can be laundered; they are more hygienic than sponges, which can house bacteria. Wash them on a hot cycle regularly, or soak them in a bleach solution to kill any germs. If you prefer to use disposable cloths, make sure that you replace them regularly.

Some washing-up liquids definitely have an adverse effect on skin so change brands until you find one that suits you. Or wear rubber gloves assiduously.

○ DO dry cutlery by hand. If left in a watery pile, it will become a hotbed for nasty bacteria.

○ DO fill really dirty saucepans with warm water and washing powder – the powder will miraculously lift burnt-on food from pans.

○ DO put rolled-up kitchen paper in damp vases or bottles and leave overnight – the paper will absorb excess moisture.

○ DO remove stains from enamel with half a lemon and some salt, or a mild bleach solution.

○ DO polish dry glasses to remove smears and spots.

○ DO hand-wash ceramics that could crack in the heat of the dishwasher, and never put very hot ceramics straight into cold water.

○ DO NOT leave knives with bone or wooden handles to soak – the handles will eventually fall apart from the blade.

Hobs and ovens

The sign of a meticulous home-keeper is a sparkling oven and hob but there are few of us who wipe them down after each and every use, and this is where the problems begin. Once grime starts to accumulate, it is annoyingly hard to tackle. To avoid getting hobs and ovens caked in grime, clean them regularly so you never get the kind of build-up that can only be shifted with highly toxic chemicals.

Keeping the hob clean should be easy: a quick wipe down after each use with a soapy cloth, and if it's particularly dirty then douse it with a kitchen spray and leave that to get to work while you get on with the washing-up. After a few minutes the surface will wipe clean painlessly. Once in a while, perhaps every fortnight or month (depending on how often you cook), give hobs a more thorough clean, taking off all the removable parts and soaking them in soapy water. When cooking, use a splatter guard: a mesh 'lid' that sits on top of pans. They come in different sizes and will prevent anything that spits, from fried foods through to tomato sauces and soups, from staining your hobs or walls.

Unless you have a zero-tolerance approach to kitchen grime, it is less likely that you will clean the oven after each use. Line the bottom of the oven with a layer of tin foil or with Lakeland's Magic Oven Liner (see above), which can be cut down to size, sits in the bottom of the oven and can be removed and cleaned easily. Lining oven shelves with foil can also save a lot of scrubbing, particularly if you are cooking something you know will make a big mess. If your oven is already covered in cooked-on debris, you will probably have to use a commercial oven cleaner. These are highly toxic, so always use rubber gloves and make sure you open nearby windows before starting. For a more natural alternative, try putting a layer of bicarbonate of soda (or baking powder) over the area, followed by a sprinkling of water. Leave it overnight and then remove the grime the next day.

The fridge

It is good to get into the habit of cleaning the fridge whenever you come home with the weekly shopping so that mould and dirt never have a chance to thrive and so that food is disposed of before it becomes a health hazard. Always remove any fresh food that is past the point of no return – that's anything dangerously past its sell-by date, anything with mould, or leftovers that will use up space before eventually being thrown out. Then remove the drawers and shelves and wash them in hot water with washing-up liquid, rinse them in very hot water and leave to air-dry while you wipe the inside of the fridge down with a hot soapy cloth. Wipe the inside down with a clean damp cloth to remove any soap residue. Really dirty fridges need a more thorough clean. The only way to remove mould is with a bleach solution and some elbow grease. Scrub until clean and then wash the insides as above.

As temperatures vary from one part of the fridge to another, it's important to store food methodically. The drawers at the bottom of your fridge are warmer than the shelves higher up, so keep perishable salads here, along with vegetables and fruit. If you need to wash very dirty vegetables, then make sure they are dry before storing them or they will rot. Remove leaves from beetroot and radishes before storing them too. Take fruit and vegetables out of plastic bags – if stored in the plastic bags, condensation will form and food will rot very quickly. The door is the warmest part of the fridge so keep less perishable drinks, dressings and condiments here, while the back of the fridge tends to be the coolest place so avoid leaving delicate herbs or soft fruits here where they could freeze. Meat and dairy products, on the other hand, will be safest at the back of the fridge.

The rest of the fridge can be arranged as you prefer, but it makes sense to store raw meat and fish on the lowest shelf to prevent any of their juices dripping and possibly contaminating other foods, although if you store them on plates this is unlikely to happen. Always keep cooked meats elsewhere in the fridge, away from raw meats. Never put hot foods straight into the fridge where they can radically reduce the overall temperature; wait for food to cool before putting it away.

○ DO try to avoid cramming the fridge with food
– it will be less efficient when full.

○ DO keep the coils at the back of the fridge clean.
A heavy build-up of dust will make your fridge
and freezer less energy-efficient.

○ DO check the temperature of your fridge and
freezer with a thermometer. The fridge should
be no more than 5°C, while the freezer should be
-18°C or less.

○ DO place a bowl of bicarbonate of soda in the fridge
– it will get rid of any lingering smells. Of course,
check what is causing the smell first and get rid of it.

The freezer

If your freezer has become a mini igloo jam-packed with glacial chunks of ice, defrost it, clean it out and start from scratch. The ice not only takes up valuable space but also makes the freezer less efficient, and it's likely to hide out-of-date food that should have been binned long ago. It's best to defrost the freezer when you have as little food as possible since you will be unable to keep the food frozen for long. Err on the side of caution and don't refreeze anything that gets the chance to defrost.

Remove everything from the freezer, unplug it and leave the door open. You can speed up the defrost by placing a bowl of hot water in the freezer, but do not be tempted to chip at the ice with a knife or anything else that could damage the freezer walls. Take away chunks of ice as they fall from the walls, then, once all the ice has been removed, wash down the interior with hot soapy water and rinse with a clean cloth. Turn the electricity back on, close the door and wait until the freezer has frosted before using it again.

○ DO wrap food well in proper freezer bags before freezing. If food is not properly wrapped, it will get white patches of freezer burn.

○ DO label food before freezing with a description and date. It is easy to forget just how long things have been frozen for, and even what they are, when faced with endless blobs that all look the same.

○ DO break up big packs of food into smaller packs before freezing.

○ DO have the seals of freezer doors replaced if they are damaged. Broken seals will let in warm air.

Equipping the kitchen

Saucepans and cookware

Good pans are an investment that should, in theory, last a life-time. They can also improve your cooking since they help prevent food getting burnt, as well as creating the right conditions (such as steady heat) for food to cook to perfection. Cheaper pans might be serviceable in the short term but they are sometimes (though not always) a false economy. Saucepans can be one of the biggest expenses in the kitchen, so if you decide to go for top quality, spend some time thinking about what is best for you first. Look through the ranges in person at a good kitchen shop so you get a feel for the designs you prefer, or research on the internet (see page 154) where you can browse and drool and plan for hours on end.

Look for solid bases that conduct and maintain heat well (they will not be susceptible to hot spots, which cause sticking and burning). Solid bases are also less likely to warp under extreme heat, are more stable to cook with and won't wobble around on the hob. Mix and match from different ranges to build a set with everything you need – complete sets of shiny new pans are incredibly seductive but don't feel that you should buy everything from one range. Consider the sort of food you cook and how many people you cook for. Good results will be harder to achieve in pans that are too small (crowded pans will steam food rather than brown it), while small amounts of food are likely to get burnt if you use a pan that's too big. Key points to consider when choosing saucepans:

● Make sure that both the handle and the weight of the pan are right for you. Some cooks prefer heavy pans, while others find a heavy one too cumbersome to work with.

● Handles that stay cool during use make cooking much easier and safer. If you want to be able to transfer pans straight to the oven, make sure handles are heatproof.

● Always check the care instructions before buying pans, and remember that even when pans can be put into the dishwasher it's not always the best way to clean them. The finish on some copper pans can be permanently tarnished by harsh dishwashers.

● A basic kit would include: one stockpot (which can double as a pasta pot); a couple of smaller saucepans; one small and one larger frying pan (one should be non-stick); a griddle pan; a decent-sized roasting tin.

● Try to buy from established manufacturers so that you will be able to add to a collection in the future; always check the guarantee, too.

● Check that lids fit snugly to the rim of the saucepan. Also check to see if some lids are interchangeable. It will save on costs (and storage space) if you don't need a costly lid for every pan.

Pan material

Stainless steel These pans are the most popular for all-round use since they offer the most plus points in comparison with other materials, and they look lovely and shiny too. Good stainless-steel pans have aluminium or copper bases that heat up quickly and maintain a steady temperature. They are non-reactive, which means they can be used to cook any type of food, and they are also easy to clean; many are dishwasher-safe too. There are professional pans with all sorts of clever design features, from detachable handles (great for tiny kitchen storage) to non-drip edges, and sleek ridgeless interiors that make cleaning easy.

Cast iron It's cumbersome to use but cast iron is great for browning meat since it can reach very high temperatures, so a skillet or grill pan is a good investment. Cast iron also retains heat brilliantly and keeps the temperature constant, which makes it ideal for slow-cooking dishes such as stews. The Le Creuset range (which has all the benefits of cast iron but is much easier to maintain and clean) includes big casserole dishes called 'cocottes' that are brilliant for braising and stewing and they come in amazing colours too (the rarely seen green is glorious). Avoid having an entire set of cast-iron pans, however – they are not the best pans for all types of cooking.

Copper This conducts heat brilliantly, which makes it great for rapid cooking. It also looks beautiful, so something like a copper roasting pan can transfer from the oven to the table.

Over time the lining can wear and will need to be replaced, and the exterior of the pans needs to be carefully cleaned using either a specialist cleaner or by rubbing with half a lemon and some salt. While many copper pans can be put into the dishwasher, hand-washing is more likely to maintain their beautiful finish.

Non-stick pans New generation non-stick pans are much more advanced than the thin, cheap non-stick pans of old. The most advanced are heavy-gauge aluminium pans with high-tech, tough, non-stick surfaces. These pans are built to

There is also sleek modern furniture designed by his son, Corin Mellor.

The ultimate kitchen shop, **Divertimenti** has an equally seductive website (*www.divertimenti.co.uk*; 020 7935 0689) featuring the same carefully sourced kitchen equipment and tableware. Everything from the best range of pans to world-famous knives is carefully sourced and you get the feeling that someone with exquisite taste has kept a watchful eye over everything sold here.

The choice of kitchen kit at **www.johnlewis.co.uk** (08456 049049) is not as extensive or as mouth-watering as the above sites but it's a good place to look for electrical equipment because the range is larger and sometimes more competitive than at other shops. It's also a great place to buy basics and, of course, other household goods too.

last and, unlike their predecessors, can withstand metal implements. They can often be transferred to the oven, too. The other benefit of non-stick pans (besides the obvious one) is that they allow you to cook using less fat.

Other cookware

Oven dishes Some sturdy dishes for stews, pot roasts and gratins are useful. Le Creuset's 'cocottes' (see page 153) are brilliant for slow-cooking meats and can go straight from oven to table. However, other earthenware or ceramic dishes are also good for cooking in the oven as they retain heat well and maintain an even cooking temperature. If a dish has a handle, check that it's the type of handle you will easily be able to hold when you are trying to lift the hot and laden dish out of the oven. Roasting tins should be solid enough to ensure that food is cooked evenly without burning and ideally they will be tough enough to be used on the hob. Always make sure that they will fit into your oven before buying them. If you plan to roast fatty birds or meat, then buy a rack to use in the tin to prevent meat stewing in its own juices.

Cake tins These are inexpensive and good ones will last for years if you look after them. Buying non-stick pans is not crucial since most cake recipes call for greased or lined tins anyway. Springform tins (the ones that pop open) are ideal for novice cake-makers who might be scared of sponges sticking, but the size and shape of tin you buy depends on what kinds of cake you intend to bake. Don't buy huge tins if you only ever make fairy cakes. If you plan to bake regularly, buy a cooling rack, which can also be used for draining fried food.

Knives

Even if you have several good, sharp knives, there is always one that feels better to work with, which you instinctively grab for most jobs. Invariably, this is because it feels more comfortable to use. So the first thing to consider when buying a new knife is how it feels: is the handle comfortable and is the knife light/heavy enough for you? When you are chopping several pounds of vegetables at one sitting, the right knife will make all the difference. Buy one at a time so you get used to using it. If you like it, go back and invest in more, but avoid buying sets of knives at all costs – more often than not there will be knives in the set that you never use.

Old-fashioned carbon-steel knives are very soft and hence easy to sharpen. They are fantastic for carving meat but need a lot of care. They rust easily so need to be cleaned and dried straight after use (though they can be oiled to avoid rusting). They can discolour food and absorb flavours; if you do use one, clean it after use by rubbing it with half a lemon.

○ DO hand-wash knives promptly and never put them to soak in water or leave them damp or the handle could be damaged or the blade get rusty.

○ DO use wooden or plastic chopping boards rather than glass or ceramic, which can damage blades.

☆

KNIVES THAT HAVE a full tang (where the blade goes right the way down through the handle in one piece) are strong and should last a lifetime. In reality, you don't need very many knives, but if you want to build a set it might include a chef's knife, a paring knife (useful for peeling smaller things like garlic and shallots when a chef's knife is too unwieldy) and a bigger serrated knife for cutting meat and slicing fruit.

O DO keep knives sharp so they work efficiently. Far more accidents are caused by blunt knives than sharp ones.

O DO wash knives separately from the rest of the washing-up. If you chuck them in the bowl with everything else they can wreak havoc on your precious glass or china, or, indeed, your precious fingers.

O DON'T store knives in a drawer full of other bits and pieces where they can get damaged or go blunt. Wooden blocks can be difficult to clean, although some are detachable for easy cleaning. A magnetic rack is probably the most convenient way to store knives – although not for fans of late-night horror films.

Other blades

Sharp kitchen scissors can be used for all sorts of things from chopping up chives or pancetta to cutting string for pieces of meat. Always make sure that kitchen scissors are washable and that they are used only in the kitchen. A good peeler is also an essential. The cheap Y-shaped ones that are sold everywhere will peel mountains of vegetables in record speed (they are more efficient than the old-style peelers), and they can be used to shave Parmesan for pasta or salads and to make scrolls of chocolate too. Box graters are much easier to use than the

KNIFE-SHARPENING TIPS

from David Mellor

USING A STEEL (METHOD 1)
Holding the steel rod vertically on a firm surface, grasp the knife low on the handle with the blade at a 20-degree angle to the steel. Bring the knife down and across the steel, drawing it towards you until the tip meets the steel at the base. Reverse the action, holding the other side of the blade against the other side of the steel, this time pushing away from you. Repeat both actions until the blade is sharp.

USING A STEEL (METHOD 2)
Grasp the steel in one hand and the knife in the other. Place the handle ends of each together, with the blade at a 20-degree angle to the steel. Raise your elbows and part your hands, making the blade travel up the steel until the tip of the blade is against the steel. Repeat, holding the other side of the blade against the other side of the steel, and continue to repeat both movements until the blade is sharp. When the edge disappears altogether, knives have to be sharpened professionally to get the edge back.

flat ones, which need to be held against another surface. Make sure you buy one that is both stable and large enough to grate big quantities of food. Mezzalunas are useful (although not at all essential) for chopping up big piles of herbs.

Chopping boards

A good solid board is another thing worth spending a bit of money on. Ideally you need a wooden board that's big enough to do lots of preparation on (the more solid it is, the more stable it will be to work on), and then a smaller one that's more transportable and useful for chopping onions and garlic. Raw meat and fish should be prepared on a separate board to avoid cross-contamination, and a plastic board that can be scrubbed clean or put into the dishwasher is usually the best option for this. Wooden boards should never be immersed in water but scrubbed thoroughly with a soapy cloth, rinsed with a clean wet cloth and then left to air-dry. If the board does become very wet it can be sprinkled with salt, which will absorb moisture. Salt crystals scrubbed in with half a lemon will clean the board and remove stains.

○ DON'T use glass or marble boards for any preparation as they will ruin good knives. If you have such a board, you will probably find it more useful for serving than for preparation.

○ DO put a damp tea towel under slipping boards.

○ DO use a special carving board for meat – channels will collect juices rather than allowing them to drip over worktops.

Other kitchen kit

Beware the kitchen gadget that's a bit like a fad diet – it seems to be the solution to all our problems but once the novelty has worn off it's soon discarded and forgotten about until the next new thing comes along. If you make bread every weekend then your bread-maker will be highly prized, but more often than not machines end up cluttering cupboards and collecting dust. Why do you need a smoothie maker when a blender will do the same job, as well as many more besides?

Multi-tasking kitchen equipment is the thing to invest in, and few machines are as versatile as a **food processor**. It will grate, chop and shred as well as mix pastry, make sauces and purée soups. A good food processor will give years, if not decades, of service so it's worth spending a lot of money on the best (which usually means the most powerful you can afford). Hand-held blenders are also useful and will save on space if you don't have room for a bigger machine. They are brilliant for soups and sauces or for puréeing smaller quantities of food.

If you plan to bake, then you need a **food mixer**, unless you have the Olympian arm muscles required to beat a mixture to fluffy perfection. Choose mixers by manufacturers such as Kenwood that have a proven track record, or the equally efficient KitchenAid, which produces fabulously retro

HOUSEHOLD FILES

THE EASIEST WAY to keep track of all the handbooks,
manuals, guarantees and receipts for household
appliances is to store them all in one big file. Buy a
ring-bound file and store all paperwork in sections
marked by the room in your home. This is also a good
place to store useful household numbers and bills too.

mixers in colours from primrose yellow to candy pink – they
alone are incentive enough to get baking. If you don't have the
space for a large mixer, a hand-held mixer is a useful alternative. The only drawback, apart from having less power, is that
it can't be left to work independently in the same way that a
proper mixer can.

Even the best **wooden spoons** (which are made from
beech) are cheap, so it's worth buying a few in different sizes.
Make sure that they have a smooth finish so they are easy to
clean; never soak them or put them in the dishwasher. A couple of large metal spoons are essential for serving food – one
should have holes for vegetables while others should be plain
for sauces, gravy, stews and so on. A good-sized ladle is also
handy, and it's essential for making risotto. Tongs, especially
the spring ones with scalloped edges, are great for turning
meat and fish or anything else that is too hot to handle.

There are many different **whisks** around but the only
one that is a kitchen must-have is a decent-sized balloon
whisk that will magically zap lumps from sauces and gravy as
well as whip up egg whites without much bother. Smaller flat

whisks are also handy for finishing sauces and for smaller quantities.

If you are a confident cook you could probably get through life without measuring much, but there are times when it is unwise to guess. You can spend anything from a few pounds on the most basic **weighing scales** to quite a lot on a state-of-the art version. Expensive digital scales that measure liquids as well as solids are much more precise and are nice to own but hardly essential – a cheap set of kitchen scales is perfectly serviceable. If you buy a metal **measuring jug**, you can use it for hot liquids as well as cold ones.

If you only want to buy one **colander** then get one large enough for draining big quantities of pasta when you are cooking for friends – the smaller ones are useless once you are cooking for more than about three or four people. A **sieve** is indispensable for baking, although if you don't plan to make cakes or pastry you could probably get by without one.

Freshly ground pepper makes a big difference to flavour. You could always grind peppercorns in a pestle and mortar or even a little electrical grinder, if you have one, and use the pepper straight from a small dish, but a **pepper mill** is not a huge expense. Electric pepper mills are popular but milling by hand gives you more control, which is useful if you are less confident about seasoning. Look for a mill that feels good to hold and use, and preferably one where you can switch from coarse to fine grinding.

A **hand-operated food mill** is the next best thing to an electric food processor, and for making sauces with texture it's actually better because you can choose whether to purée to a fine, medium or coarse texture. They only cost a few pounds and are handy for making proper tomato sauces for pasta or for soups. A good **masher** needs to be ergonomic if you are going to get your mash perfectly fluffy and light (Good Grips make a brilliant one), or use a potato ricer for super-smooth mash.

A **salad spinner** – a sort of big plastic bowl with an inner bowl that spins and drains salad leaves – sounds like the sort of thing that could languish for years in the back of a cupboard, but it really is useful and only costs a few pounds. The only way to successfully dress a salad is if the leaves are dry – leave them wet and the oily dressing will never cling on.

Mixing bowls are one of those things you can't have too many of, especially if you are preparing a lot of food or cooking ahead of time. Different materials obviously have different plus points. Metal bowls are useful for decanting hot liquids into, although if you have a metal measuring jug you could use that instead. Plastic can go straight into the microwave, while a big ceramic bowl provides a good stable surface if you are mixing pastry or similar, and looks great too. This is one of the few times when buying a set does make sense, since you will almost certainly use all of them at some point.

Cooking

The basics of shopping, and storing and preparing food

CONTRARY TO WHAT YOU MAY THINK, anyone can make something delicious to eat. You don't need an encyclopaedic knowledge of technique or a kitchen full of flashy kit. You don't need hours of preparation time, and you certainly don't need a shelf groaning under the weight of glossy cookbooks (although some, of course, are very useful). The logical way for new cooks, and most other cooks, to make good food is to buy the very best ingredients and then do as little to them as possible. Keeping things simple will make your life so much easier. From the shopping to the preparation and serving, the pared-down approach to cooking will be a revelation to anyone terrorized by tricky recipes and dinner-party nightmares.

Shopping well is the first step. Ideally, we would all have a food market on our doorstep, with a baker producing startlingly good bread, a rosy-cheeked butcher selling organic meat, a fantastic fish stall brimming with the daily catch. While farmer's markets are making this kind of shopping increasingly possible (find one near you by contacting the **Soil Association**: *www.soilassociation.org*; 0117 929 0661), for most of us, the supermarket is still where we end up doing the weekly shop. But a bit of shopping savvy will allow you to make the most of the big stores, and then you can cherry-pick from smaller specialists for treats whenever you have the time or money.

Of course, buying the best possible produce doesn't guarantee good results, but by getting to grips with a few key rules you can quickly become an accomplished cook. It's about understanding ingredients – learning about seasoning combining flavours and textures and developing a sense of what works. It's also about planning and organization. If you feel on top of it all, you are far less likely to get flustered and make mistakes.

These days we are a pretty schizophrenic bunch when it comes to cooking. Sometimes, perhaps most of the time, we want to throw something together in a matter of minutes, while at other times we want to spend most of the weekend shopping, cooking and eating. But however you cook, the same basic principles apply, and once you have a grasp of them, you will become confident and able in the kitchen.

Getting organized

Listening to many contemporary food writers and chefs, you would imagine that it's easy to pop along to the market, throwing together a little menu as you go along, gathering good produce from whatever is plentiful and seasonal. For anyone with a headful of ideas and recipes this is fine, but for most of us, and certainly for anyone intimidated by cooking, it makes no sense at all.

Most of us need the help of a well-thought-out list. If you are cooking for others, then you need to devise a menu. Do it well ahead of the day so you have time to sort out a plan of action; trying to squeeze in a frantic supermarket trolley dash between work and supper will leave you frazzled before you've cooked a thing. Hosts who seem inconceivably calm have usually spent a great deal of time planning a menu, doing the shopping and getting ahead.

Getting food prepared in advance can alleviate much last-minute stress, and certainly makes a lot of sense if you have several guests coming for lunch or dinner. Try to get at least one course completely organized ahead of time, or at least the main components of it. Prepare vegetables in the morning before you go to work, or even the night before. If there's a lot of fiddly preparation to be done, get most of this out of the way too; everything does not need to be chopped and arranged, telly-chef-style, in little glass bowls, but get most of the preparation work done ahead so that you don't get flustered later on.

Cooking with an audience can also be unnerving, which is another reason to get work done before friends arrive. You need to be incredibly confident to cook in front of a group of guests, and they are bound to distract you with some sizzling gossip just as your garlic burns to a frazzle. It's also much easier to rectify things if you don't have someone breathing down your neck.

While there is less chance of anything going wrong if you are calm and organized, do accept that occasionally things don't go according to plan. Everyone has cooking disasters, so don't be too intimidated by them – the trick is to try to figure out what went wrong so you get it right next time, rather than giving up altogether. One way to build up confidence is to master one thing at a time. A risotto might seem daunting, for example, but after a few attempts, perhaps with varying results, you'll realize just how simple it really is. As you build confidence, so you'll be able to take a few ingredients and whip up delicious food without even glancing at a cookbook.

○ DO use the internet if you don't have time to get to the shops. Either order your groceries from supermarkets that offer delivery or from smaller producers who usually deliver by overnight courier.

○ DO, if you are cooking for a group of people, plan to cook things where there is as little last-minute cooking as possible. Doing one or two things just before serving is manageable, but juggling complex procedures creates havoc even in the most orderly kitchen.

○ DO keep your store cupboard full of basics to reduce last-minute panics.

The store cupboard

A well-stocked store cupboard is a good thing. With the right ingredients to hand you will always be able to throw something together, even if you haven't had a chance to go shopping all week. It's also comforting and reassuring knowing that you have all the ingredients you need plus a few treats nestling in the dark corners of the kitchen. It's sensible to keep cupboards orderly and stocked up with the type of things you will actually use.

Avoid buying novelties just because they look quite interesting. They will languish for years before finally being thrown out during a spring clean or when you move house.

Also steer clear of food souvenirs, such as pots of preserved lemons bought in Morocco or big bags of cloves from Zanzibar, unless they are ingredients you already use in quantity. Otherwise, like many a holiday ornament, they simply collect dust back at home.

Try not to cram shelves with row upon row of tins and packets; it will take twice as long to find anything, and by the time you finally uncover some designer-label pasta sauce, you'll discover that it's past its sell-by date.

Tailor your supplies to what you cook. If you make a Thai curry every week, then you will need all the basics for that. Also think about things from which you can construct a simple meal if you haven't had time to shop. Here is a list of things for the store-cupboard and fridge that you probably shouldn't be without.

Olive oil If you use it regularly, get one good extra virgin oil for salads and pasta and one cheaper olive oil for general cooking.

Unsalted butter keeps in the fridge for ages (if it's unopened) and it's always useful for impromptu baking, for sauces, for sublime mash, or for slathering over toast as a weekend treat.

Maldon sea salt and **black peppercorns** These are absolute essentials.

Eggs These worth having to hand for baking days and, of course, to throw together an omelette.

Red wine vinegar Use this for salad dressings and sauces.

Parmesan Good pasta with a drizzle of extra virgin olive oil and some Parmesan is about as simple a supper as can be, but make sure you've got the real thing from an Italian deli or a really good cheese shop, and avoid dry, ready-grated supermarket Parmesan at all costs.

Mustard Use this for salad dressings, sauces and sandwiches.

Onions and garlic should always be on hand.

Lemons are almost as important as onions and garlic.

Olives A jar of fat olives will keep for ages and you can give them to friends to munch pre-dinner if you don't have anything more substantial.

Pasta Have at least one long pasta, such as spaghetti, tagliatelle or linguine, and one short type, such as penne or fusilli.

Stock Unless you always have freshly made stock in the fridge (highly unlikely), keep some good-quality stock cubes to hand.

Tinned tomatoes are good for making simple pasta sauces.

Pancetta or good bacon Handy to have in the freezer as it defrosts quickly and is useful for pasta sauces, salads or even risottos.

Baking supplies If you make cakes, biscuits or pies on a whim, it's worth always keeping stocked up with flour, caster sugar and perhaps some ground almonds.

Rice Risotto is the ultimate store-cupboard comfort food. Keep Arborio or Carnaroli for risottos, and some basmati if you plan to cook curries.

Bread Keep a loaf of really good bread in the freezer. Sliced bread will defrost quickly and can even be toasted from frozen. Keep a jar of **tapenade** and you will also have something to munch on with drinks if friends descend on you.

Chocolate Have a really good quality bar, such as Green & Black's. If you are faced with an impromptu supper with friends, this can replace pudding.

Flavour

Perhaps the key to cooking well is understanding flavour, and if you love eating this should be an easy enough skill to develop. Good ingredients are the foundation for cooking something delicious, but knowing what to do with them and how to bring out their flavour is just as important. In other words, even if you buy the very best ingredients and follow a recipe to the letter, what you cook can still taste mediocre if you don't match ingredients well and season judiciously. Seasoning doesn't just mean salt and pepper, although good use of salt and pepper is important.

Get into the habit of tasting while you cook and always do a final check, adjusting the seasoning where necessary. Some foods, such as tomatoes, potatoes and pasta, need more salt than you might think. But most foods need some help – salt (and usually pepper) can turn something quite bland into something delicious. Just think about mashed potato, which, if seasoned correctly (and, of course, mashed to a delicious fluff), is sublime, but without salt and pepper tastes quite dull. Knowing how, when and why to season is a skill that's well worth nurturing. Even amongst professional chefs a knack for seasoning can be missing. You can only develop the knack through experience, and there's an awful lot of personal choice in all this too.

○ DO use good salt, such as Maldon sea salt, and always use freshly ground black pepper, unless a recipe calls specifically for another kind.

○ DO pay attention to when you season – if a recipe tells you to season during cooking or at the end, there is usually a good reason for it.

○ DON'T season meat long before cooking – salt can draw out moisture from meat so it's best to season immediately before or during cooking.

○ DO go easy on the salt when seasoning a dish that contains bacon, stock cubes, cheese or anything else with a high salt content of its own.

○ DO, if you have oversalted a stew or casserole,
add some chunks of raw potato, which should
absorb much of the salt while they cook.

Of course, there's a lot more to seasoning than just salt and
pepper – using fresh herbs, spices, lemons and aromatics will
make a huge difference to your cooking. Sometimes a recipe
calls for the simplest flavouring, but other foods benefit from
a complex mixture of tastes. Think about a slowly cooked stew
that may have onions, garlic, a handful of woody herbs and
some fried pancetta added for flavour. As you cook more, you
quickly develop a sense of how to build flavour. Your own
tastes should govern whether something works for you or not,
although there are a few irrefutable combinations. Perhaps a
good idea when starting out is to focus on these marriages.
Chicken escalopes marinated in plenty of olive oil, lemon
juice, salt and pepper and then cooked quickly on a hot grill
pan make a quick and delicious meal, for example. A tomato
sauce for pasta flavoured only with some fragrant basil leaves
is another example of two basic ingredients exquisitely
matched. You will feel more confident about straying from
recipes and throwing in a bit of this or that once these combinations have become second nature.

Here are some natural affinities you can't go wrong with:

Basil – tomatoes and tomato sauce for pasta

Bay leaves – stews and braises, beef, pork

Coriander – chicken, fish, Thai curries

Dill – fish

Garlic – lamb, chicken, beef; and in stews and casseroles

Lemons – fish, chicken, lamb

Mint – new potatoes, lamb, peas (and it's crucial for Pimms and mojitos)

Parsley – fish (and it's a key ingredient of salsa verde and tabbouleh)

Rosemary – lamb, chicken, fish

Sage – veal, pork

Tarragon – chicken

Thyme – lamb, pork, chicken; and in stews and casseroles

Often the first stages of cooking are the most important, since this is where you begin to build up flavours. Anyone can fry an onion, but knowing how to cook onions and garlic is probably a little more refined than you think. If a recipe tells you to slowly caramelize onions or shallots, take your time and let them gently fry until they are glistening and golden. This makes all the difference to the final flavour, creating sweeter and richer sauces, stews or whatever else you are cooking. Likewise, the taste of garlic varies wildly: cooked really quickly it has a strong flavour, but cooked gently and slowly it will be mild and sweet.

As a general rule, woody herbs such as rosemary, bay and thyme are added early in the cooking process because they can take intense or long, slow cooking. Leafier herbs such as basil, parsley, tarragon or coriander are added later in the cooking or at the very end as they are too delicate to withstand much heat. Because woody herbs are fairly robust, the dried form can be as useful as the fresh, but for leafy herbs you should only ever use fresh.

Heat

The thought of burning food to an inedible charcoal crisp is probably what scares new cooks the most, so a basic under-standing of when to jack up the heat and cook food in a few minutes or when to use the gentlest heat possible is something you need to develop. It depends on what you want to cook. With meat, the cut largely dictates how it needs to be treated. Expensive prime cuts of meat are usually more tender and often leaner; they can be cooked quickly at moderate to high temperatures in a frying pan or on a grill until the outside is browned while the inside is juicy and tender. This method is a quick and simple way to cook chicken, meaty fish and vegetables too. This kind of cooking requires attention, so this is not the time to get sucked into your favourite telly soap. Conversely, tougher, cheaper cuts of meats need cooking at a gentle temperature over a long period of time. Delicate fish, whether it is cooked in the oven or on the hob, requires a gentle to moderate heat and a very short cooking time.

How hot should your pan be? There are all sorts of ways to judge the temperature when cooking. Meat or fish should sizzle when added to a frying pan or grill. If it makes no noise, then the pan and the oil or other fat are not hot enough. If it spits ferociously, then the pan is probably too hot and you should remove it from the heat for a minute to let it cool a little. This rule can also be applied to browning onions, garlic and other vegetables. If there is no initial sizzle, your pan needs to get hotter. If you want to fry onions or other vegetables gently until they are soft and transparent rather than golden brown, however, you don't need such a hot pan and you shouldn't get the initial sizzle.

Equally, there is a considerable difference between various water temperatures, and you should learn to recognize a steady simmer (for more delicate vegetables), a more rapid boil (for hardy root vegetables) and a ferocious rolling boil (the temperature at which pasta needs to be added to a pan).

○ DO use your sense of smell. When food is coming to the end of its cooking time, you will be able to smell it. A cake, for example, will fill the house with a home-baking waft.

○ DO add a little oil when frying in butter – butter easily burns if used on its own.

○ DO keep a close eye on what you are cooking – it is the easiest way to keep the food at the right temperature.

○ DO bear in mind that a small amount of food in a large pan, either on the hob or in the oven, will catch or burn more quickly.

How much to cook

Knowing how much to cook for yourself is simple enough, but when you are faced with cooking for six or eight or even more, quantities can throw you into a bit of a panic. With experience it becomes easy to judge, but if you are a novice, follow the rough guidelines below. There are also a few things to bear in mind. People nearly always eat more than you would imagine, especially men, and it's far better to have too much food than too little – you don't want to find yourself worrying that you don't have enough and praying no one will ask for a bigger serving. Similarly, always make more pudding than you think you need – it always gets eaten.

Meat and chicken 225g/8oz per person or, if you are buying meat on the bone, allow 340g/12oz for meat and 450g/1lb for chicken. Butchers usually have a pretty accurate idea of how much you will need, so ask for their advice too.

Fish 170g/6oz for fillets or steaks, or allow 340–450g/12oz–1lb per person for whole fish. For shellfish, allow 85g/3oz per person for a starter and 140g/5oz per person for a main. Use smaller quantities, about 110g/4oz, for cured fish such as smoked salmon.

Vegetables 110g/4oz per person if serving another vegetable.

Potatoes 170g/6oz per person if serving mashed or steamed potatoes, and allow three or four roast potatoes each.

Rice 55g/2oz (dry weight) per person unless as part of a main dish, such as a risotto, when you need 85g/3oz per person.

Pasta 55g/2oz (dry weight) for a starter and 110g/4oz for a main per person.

ORGANIC SUPPLIERS

If you don't have access to a local farm shop or farmer's market, then order meat, game and fish via internet shops. For more information on organic suppliers nationwide, contact the Soil Association (*www.soilassociation.org*; 0117 929 0661).

Northfield Farm: (01664 474271; *www.northfieldfarm.com*).They will deliver their excellent naturally reared beef, pork and lamb by overnight courier. Also have a stall at south London's Borough Market every Friday and Saturday.

Swaddles: (0845 456 1768; *www.swaddles.co.uk*). They will deliver organic meat including sausages, bacon and ready-cooked meals by overnight courier. They also deliver by van every week in London, Surrey and Middlesex.

Wild Meat Company: (01728 663211; *www.wildmeat.co.uk*). Seasonal game birds, venison and rabbit reared on farms and estates in East Anglia, as well as grouse from Yorkshire. Delivery by overnight courier.

Graig Farm: (01597 851655; *www.graigfarm.co.uk*). Meat, poultry and game as well as wild and farmed fish. The online shop also supplies fruit and vegetable boxes and bread.

Cooking from the store cupboard

Pasta and rice are the linchpins of store-cupboard cooking. Both can be made into delicious (and economical) basic dishes, using ingredients you have to hand, and then embellished and elaborated on. Risottos and pasta dishes are the ultimate comfort foods that can easily be tarted up with flashy, luxurious twists. And being able to whip up a feast with ingredients you happen to have in will seem like a culinary conjuring trick to unexpected guests. The only addition should be a perfectly dressed, crisp green salad.

Basic risotto for 4

1tbsp olive oil
110g/4oz butter
2 small onions or a few shallots, finely chopped
1 clove garlic, finely chopped
1 stick celery, finely chopped
340g/12oz Arborio or Carnaroli rice
1 glass white wine or vermouth
900ml/1½ pints of vegetable stock, simmering
     gently in a separate pan
110g/4oz Parmesan, freshly grated

Heat the olive oil and half the butter, then add the onion, garlic and celery and fry gently until soft – this will take about 6 or 7 minutes.

Add the rice and stir well, allowing to heat through and absorb all the juices and oils in the pan. (Rather than measuring the rice, you can just add a couple of small handfuls per person.)

Add the wine and continue to cook for 1–2 minutes. The pan should be hot enough so that the liquid is bubbling and reducing down.

Now add a ladleful of hot stock and stir into the rice over a medium heat. Wait until most of the liquid is absorbed, which will take a couple of minutes, then add another ladle of stock. Continue stirring and adding stock until the risotto starts to look creamy and the rice is almost cooked but with a slight bite. This should take about 15–20 minutes. Season with salt and pepper, add the Parmesan and the rest of the butter, and leave to sit for a minute with the lid on the pan. Then stir and serve immediately.

This is the basic recipe for risotto, but it can also be tailored to what you have available. Here are some variations.

- Add saffron to the stock to make a rich golden Risotto Milanese.

- Stir in any parboiled green vegetables, such as asparagus tips, wilted spinach, fresh peas or broad beans, at the end of the cooking, giving them time to heat through.

- Use herbs, such as chopped basil, which is delicious with the zest and juice of a lemon added at the end of cooking. Or stir in lemon thyme leaves before adding the stock and then some crumbled goat's cheese at the end of cooking.

● Add dried porcini to make a mushroom risotto. Soak the porcini in hot water for 30 minutes and add the liquor to the stock. Chop the porcini and mix into the rice before adding the stock.

Pasta dishes

There are, quite literally, hundreds of different ways to serve pasta. Sauces range from the most basic drizzle of really good olive oil to rich, slowly cooked meat ragus. Here are a few of the most basic.

Take a bowlful of freshly grated **Parmesan** and stir in the juice of two **lemons**, several glugs of good olive oil and some torn basil leaves. Mix together, season and pour over freshly cooked spaghetti or linguine. Mix well and serve. (Keep lemons out of the fridge so they are easier to squeeze.)

Soften some onions and garlic in olive oil until they are golden, then add peeled and chopped fresh plum **tomatoes** or a tin of finely chopped tomatoes and leave to simmer until the sauce is thick and reduced. Season well, add some torn basil leaves and stir into freshly cooked penne.

Stir deli-bought fresh **pesto** into freshly cooked spaghetti.

Melt about 100g/4oz of **gorgonzola** into about 50g/2oz of butter over a gentle heat and stir well. Add a few tablespoons of double cream and heat through before stirring into freshly cooked pasta.

PASTA TIPS

from Antonio Carluccio

Always cook pasta in a large saucepan – allow 1 litre of water per 100g of pasta.

Add salt (allowing 2tsp per litre of water) just before adding the pasta.

Pasta should always be added to water that has reached a rolling boil. Once you have added the pasta, put the lid on the saucepan until the water is boiling again then leave the lid off for the rest of the cooking time.

Don't add oil to the water unless you are cooking sheets of pasta (such as lasagne), and never rinse the pasta once it is cooked.

Drain in a large colander, add sauce and serve immediately.

A relaxed Saturday lunch

Weekend cooking should be languorous and relaxing, allowing for haphazard timings – apart from the Sunday roast or a formal supper, of course. Cooking something in one pot, ahead of time, is one way to host an easy-going weekend lunch or supper, so if you have an evening free the day before then make a classic fish pie or shepherd's pie and reheat it on the day. Alternatively, roast a chicken that has been coated in butter and plenty of salt and pepper and serve with a green salad. Cook food that is homely, straightforward and quickly assembled, with just a few components.

Bangers and mash for 4

> pork sausages – 2 or 3 per person
> butter or oil for cooking
> 2 medium onions, finely sliced
> 1 tbsp flour
> 300ml/½ pint beef or vegetable stock
> 1 glass red wine (optional)
> Worcestershire sauce or grainy mustard (optional)
>
> **For the mash:**
> 1kg/2¼ lb floury potatoes (King Edward, Maris Piper
>   or Desiree)
> 110g/4oz butter

The way to make truly sublime bangers and mash is to find really tasty sausages that will create lots of delicious juices while they are cooking in the pan – these will form the basis for a fantastic onion gravy. Buy pork sausages (sausages made from beef, venison or other meat are never quite the same) from a good butcher or choose one of the most upmarket supermarket versions.

Melt a little butter or oil in a pan over a medium heat and then add the sausages. Leave for about 4 minutes until they are golden brown, then turn them. Continue to cook and turn them. After about 15–20 minutes, the sausages should be deep brown on all sides.

While the sausages are cooking, prepare the potatoes for the mash. Peel them and chop them into halves, or quarters if they are very large. Put into a saucepan and cover with cold water and a teaspoon of salt and bring to the boil. Cook until tender, which will take about 20 minutes.

Meanwhile, remove the sausages from the pan (and preferably keep them warm in the oven), throw the onions in and fry until they are soft and golden. Sprinkle the flour over the onion and stir well until there are no lumps, scraping up all the juices and golden gloop left from the sausages. Pour the stock into the pan and simmer, stirring well. The flour will slowly thicken the gravy. You can also add some red wine, a glug or two of Worcestershire sauce or some grainy mustard. Once the sauce has thickened, taste, then season with salt and pepper.

When the potatoes are tender, strain well, allowing all the steam to evaporate so they are as dry as possible. Melt the butter in the pan, add plenty of freshly ground pepper and return the potatoes to the pan. Mash well until all lumps are removed. Taste and add salt until the seasoning is perfect.

○ DO, for even fluffier potatoes, boil them in their skins and then peel before mashing.

○ DO add a little warm milk for creamier mash.

○ DO add a spoon of grainy French mustard to the mash to serve with bangers.

Sunday roasts

There are lots of different elements to think about here, so the secret to getting it right, for beginners at least, is to embark on a plan of almost military precision. If you time everything immaculately, the roast can be surprisingly stress-free and a lot less trouble than you might imagine. First, spend some time deciding what to cook. It doesn't get much more basic, or mouth-wateringly delicious, than roast chicken, and it's worth spending money on a good organic bird – they are now available at virtually all supermarkets, butchers and farmer's markets. If you plan to roast red meat, ask your butcher for advice on choosing a joint.

○ DO buy well-hung beef – it will have more flavour and a better texture than most of the bright-red supermarket equivalents. Look for a deep-red meat with a good marbling of pale fat, which will keep it moist during cooking.

TIMINGS

Chicken Cook for 20 minutes per lb (450g) plus 25 minutes at 200°C/gas mark 6.

Beef Cook for 20 minutes at 230°C/gas mark 8 to brown. Then at 15 minutes per lb (450g) for rare, 20 minutes for medium, 25 for well done at 180°C/gas mark 4.

Lamb Cook for 20 minutes at 220°C/gas mark 7 to brown. Then at 15 minutes per lb (450g) for medium, 20 minutes for well done at 190°C/gas mark 5.

Pork For a crackling roast cook for 25 minutes per lb (450g) at 200°C/gas mark 6 plus 20 minutes.

Venison Cook for 15 minutes at 230°C/gas mark 8, then 15 minutes per lb (450g) at 200°C/gas mark 6.

O DO always preheat the oven in good time so that it's fully hot before the meat goes in.

O DO make sure that meat or chicken is at room temperature when it goes into the oven.

O DO think about the shape of what you are cooking – thick pieces of meat will take longer to cook than longer, narrow ones.

○ DO, if you are cooking something very greasy such as lamb or goose, put it on a grid or rack, which will help heat circulate and will stop the meat stewing in its own fat.

For roast chicken Make sure the skin is dry and then slather the skin with butter, coarse sea salt and freshly ground black pepper and put half a lemon inside the cavity. For extra flavour mix some chopped garlic and thyme into the butter too.

For roast lamb Make slits all over the skin and fill with small sprigs of rosemary and a sliver of garlic then season all over with coarse sea salt and freshly ground black pepper and drizzle with olive oil.

For pork crackling Make sure that the skin is very dry and then score diagonal lines about a centimetre apart all across the joint. Cut through the skin and the fat but not the meat and try to avoid your own fingers. Now season all over with plenty of coarse sea salt and freshly ground black pepper. Add some rosemary or thyme to the pan for extra flavour.

○ DO always use a good, solid roasting pan so there is even heat. A flimsy pan will buckle and is more likely to burn whatever you are cooking. A solid pan will also be able to sit on the hob so you can make the gravy.

○ DO make sure the pan is not too crowded (or food will not brown), but also make sure that meat is not dwarfed by an oversized pan (or it might burn).

Work out rough cooking times, and allow for resting time of about 20 minutes at the end of cooking, then preheat the oven. Once the oven is hot enough, put the (room-temperature) meat in. Now it can be left alone – unless you are cooking chicken, which you should baste once or twice (spooning the juices over the bird to keep it moist) after, say, 35 minutes.

Work out a rough plan for the vegetables. Potatoes need to be parboiled for 10 minutes or so, then drained well. Put them back in the saucepan and, holding the lid firmly, give them a vigorous shake to rough them up a bit, then season with salt. If there is plenty of fat in the roasting tin, cook them there for around 50 minutes, turning occasionally. Alternatively, cook them in a separate tin but heat up some lard or goose fat in it until it's very hot before adding the potatoes. Most other vegetables can be done when you remove the meat from the oven, unless you are doing root vegetables, such as parsnips, which need more time to cook.

The slightly frantic, final 20 minutes
Because you have calculated cooking times, you will know roughly when to remove the meat from the oven. However, these timings are only a guide, since the shape of the joint will also affect the time it takes to cook. To test chicken, stick in a

SALAD TIPS

LOOK FOR crisp leaves and store them in the salad drawer of your fridge. Never leave them at the back of the fridge where they can freeze.

ALWAYS MAKE SURE that salad leaves are dry or the dressing will not cling to them. Dressing should not end up in a pool at the bottom of the bowl.

STURDY, BITTER LEAVES such as chicory or frisée will stand up to thicker dressings or one made with hot chunks of pancetta, say.

DON'T DRESS SALADS until the moment before they are eaten – the dressing will wilt the leaves in minutes.

A DRESSING MUST BE emulsified to coat the leaves. Always use roughly three parts oil to one part acid (lemon juice, vinegar) and then season and add whatever else you like (some crushed garlic, mustard, some chopped herbs or shallots).

FLAVOURED OILS can be too overpowering, so stick to a good peppery olive oil for dressings.

knife and see if the juices run clear. For other meat, unless you are quite confident about knowing when it is cooked, it is probably best to use a meat thermometer. The centre of the meat should measure as follows: 60°C for rare, 70°C for medium, 80°C for well done.

This stage is really the only time you will have to juggle a little bit, but the clever thing about the roast is that everything works in your favour – the meat should now be left to rest for 20 minutes, giving you plenty of time to cook the Yorkshire puddings, make gravy, boil and drain vegetables, etc. Do not leave the meat near a draught and, if necessary, put some foil over the top to keep it from cooling.

Gravy and vegetables

Don't even think about reaching for a pot of tasteless instant gravy – making your own is far better and just as quick. Once you have put the meat aside for resting, pour off the excess fat from the cooking juices, then place the tin on a medium heat on the hob and start to scrape up all the crispy bits at the bottom. If you want a thicker gravy, add a level dessertspoon of flour and stir in well and very quickly until the lumps are removed and the flour is mixed into all the juices. Throw in a glass each of wine (red for beef, lamb or venison and white for pork or chicken) and stock (or two of stock if you prefer) and mix thoroughly, stirring all the time until the gravy thickens.

Alternatively, in place of the flour, whisk in some cubes of cold butter at the end of reducing the gravy for a thinner, glossier result.

• Put root vegetables (carrots, potatoes, swede, celeriac, etc.) into salted cold water and bring to the boil. Cook until tender.

• Add green vegetables (broccoli, cabbage, peas, etc.) to boiling water and cook without a lid. Cook so that they retain a bit of a bite.

• Refreshing green vegetables (broad beans, French beans, mangetout, spinach, etc.) in ice-cold water will stop them cooking and also helps to maintain their colour. They can be reheated quickly before serving.

A basic cake

Making a cake is not only straightforward but also takes only about 15 minutes – the rest of the time it's quietly doing its thing in the oven. And if you follow instructions carefully – and this is one of the few times in cooking when you really must – little can go wrong. You could easily buy a cake but how much nicer is it to cheer up a friend by baking her a dense chocolate cake, or making a tray of pretty flower-topped fairy cakes for a tea party. There's something deeply comforting about a home-baked cake, and it probably has a lot to do with our childhood memories of the impressiveness of a thickly iced birthday cake.

This is a basic recipe but it can be tarted up in any number of ways. Add the juice of half a lemon and some zest

WHERE TO BUY CHEESE

Neal's Yard Dairy (6 Park Street, Borough Market, London SE1; 020 7645 3550; *www.nealsyarddairy.com*). One of London's best cheese shops sells a delicious selection of British cheeses via mail order, which is particularly useful at Christmas when queues wind down the street. The shop also stocks bread from artisan bakers and is worth a visit if only for the knowledgeable and friendly staff – and to taste the cheese, of course. Mail order.

Paxton and Whitfield (3 John Street, Bath; 01225 466 403; *www.paxtonandwhitfield.co.uk*.) With royal warrants and over 200 years in business, this traditional cheesemongers stocks all the British classics you would expect alongside international cheeses. The London shop nestles among St James's shirt-makers at 93 Jermyn Street, SW1; 020 7930 0259. Mail order.

La Fromagerie (30 Highbury Park, London N5; 020 7359 7440; *www.lafromagerie.co.uk*.) This is where food writers including Nigel Slater, Nigella Lawson and Jamie Oliver come for a huge selection of sublime cheeses. The owner Patricia Michelson has even written a book on the subject. Although there is no official mail order set up, the shop will sometimes do postal deliveries.

and you have a lemon cake for tea. Substitute 30g/1oz cocoa for flour and you have a chocolate cake. Slather the whole thing when cool with a chocolate ganache – melt a bar of good dark chocolate, add it to 200ml/7fl oz double cream and mix until thick and glossy – and you have a pretty impressive pudding.

Basic sponge

> 225g/8oz softened unsalted butter
> 225g/8oz caster sugar
> 4 large eggs
> 225g/8oz self-raising flour

Preheat the oven to 180°C/gas mark 4. Grease the inside of two sandwich tins using the wrapper from the butter and then dust with a little flour. Tap off excess.

Beat the butter and sugar together until light and fluffy – it should turn almost white. If you don't have a food mixer, stop when you feel your beating arm is about to fall off. Beat the eggs together in a cup and pour into the mixture. Sieve the flour on top of this then gently stir the whole thing together. Spoon evenly into the tins and smooth over. Put them into the middle of the oven, close the door gently and leave for 25 minutes. Do not open the door.

The delicious smell of cake should waft around the kitchen when the cake is cooked, but check by pressing the top of the cake – the surface should bounce back if it's done. Or push a sharp knife into the cake and it should come out clean – if it emerges covered in goo, the cake is not ready.

Turn out gently onto a rack – you may need to run a knife around the edges to ease it out – and leave to cool. Sandwich together with jam and dust with icing sugar. Or fill with mounds of whipped cream and strawberries, or any other soft fruit for that matter.

Choosing cookbooks

Glossy cookbooks are used as much for inspiration and pure indulgence as actually learning to cook, but there are a few contemporary writers whose books are must-haves for any-one starting out. Nigel Slater (for common-sense advice and mouth-watering recipe writing), Nigella Lawson (everyone should own her first and best book, *How to Eat*) and Jamie Oliver (workable recipes written in a friendly, approachable way) are a sort of kitchen holy trinity. They seem to under-stand when, how and what we all want to cook at home. This is not to say that cheffy tomes should be ignored, but don't try to cook from them and then feel a failure if you can't get to grips with complex sauces, long recipes and trying to recreate the glistening towers in their pages.

Delia Smith was, for good reason, the best-loved cookery writer before Jamie could even reach his KitchenAid. Her *Complete Cookery Course* is worth owning if only because sometimes we all want to look up the definitive recipe for Yorkshire puddings or Madeira cake. Equally, writers such as Jane Grigson (for classic English cooking) and Elizabeth David (for her insights into French and Mediterranean food) are both sensible additions to your cookbook shelf. Elizabeth David also has the most delicious chocolate cake recipe in her best-known book, *French Provincial Cooking*.

○ DO always read a recipe from start to finish and make sure you have all the ingredients before beginning.

○ DO think about how time-consuming each element is in a recipe. Sometimes instructions can seem quite simple but are actually fairly work-intensive.

○ DO remember that recipes are not always written in stone – use cooking times as a guide but be aware that all ovens vary.

○ DON'T be fooled by photography. The end result will not necessarily look the same as the picture in the cookbook.

Cooking jargon explained

Bain-marie Where food is gently cooked in one bowl or dish sitting in another dish or saucepan half filled with hot water. Often used to bake custards or terrines in the oven or for cooking a delicate sauce or melting chocolate on the hob.

Bake blind To cook a pastry case for a tart before adding the filling. The bottom is prevented from bubbling up and the case kept in shape by being filled with ceramic beans or dried beans, and cooked until lightly golden.

Baste To spoon juice or fat over food while it is being cooked, most commonly when roasting meat or vegetables.

Blanch Brief boiling to part-cook vegetables such as spinach or beans that simply need to be reheated before serving.

Boil Hopefully everyone knows how to boil water, but you should also learn to recognize a rolling boil, which is as hot as water needs to be before cooking pasta, and a gentle simmer, in which to cook more delicate vegetables.

Braise Slow cooking meat with liquid and vegetables, usually in the oven.

Browning Recipes often call for meat and chicken to be browned before the main cooking. Keep the heat quite high, and do not crowd the pan or you will create too much steam and prevent the meat from browning.

Coulis A thick sauce, usually made from berries that have been puréed.

Cream To beat ingredients together with a wooden spoon or in a food mixer.

Deglaze To add liquid, usually wine, stock or water, to a pan after grilling, frying or roasting to lift off the caramelized bits and combine them with the juices and fats into a sauce.

Emulsify To blend a fat and another liquid together, such as mixing oil and vinegar together for a dressing.

En croute Cooking in a pastry case.

En papillote Baking something, usually fish, wrapped in paper or foil.

Escalope A flattened piece of meat.

Flambé To set food alight using alcohol.

Fold To mix ingredients together by turning over gently with a metal spoon. Usually for delicate cake mixes, meringues, etc.

Marinate To soak ingredients in liquid such as alcohol, juice, oil or vinegar, along with herbs or other flavourings, before cooking. Overnight for pieces of meat or merely minutes for delicate pieces of fish.

Parboil Part-cooking vegetables either before roasting or so that they simply need to be reheated before serving.

Reduce To boil or simmer a liquid until it is reduced in volume. As its water content evaporates, the flavour intensifies.

Refresh Putting vegetables into cold water to stop them cooking.

Relax Leaving food such as pastry, batter or meat to rest before cooking.

Sealing Usually refers to meat that needs to be seared on all sides on a high heat before the main cooking.

Sweating Gently cooking something so that it doesn't brown but slowly cooks. Usually refers to onions or shallots.

Conversion Tables

OVEN TEMPERATURES

°C	Gas	°F
140	1	275
150	2	300
170	3	325
180	4	350
190	5	375
200	6	400
220	7	425
230	8	450
240	9	475

LIQUID MEASURES

28ml	1fl oz	2 tbsp
56ml	2fl oz	4 tbsp
150ml	5fl oz	1/4 pint
190ml	6.6fl oz	1/3 pint
290ml	10fl oz	1/2 pint
425ml	15fl oz	3/4 pint
570ml	20fl oz	1 pint

WEIGHT CONVERSIONS

15g	½oz	200g	7oz	400g	14oz
30g	1oz	225g	8oz	425g	15oz
55g	2oz	255g	9oz	450g	1lb
85g	3oz	285g	10oz	900g	2lb
110g	4oz	310g	11oz	1kg	2¼lb
140g	5oz	340g	12oz		
170g	6oz	370g	13oz		

Entertaining

*The stress-free way to plan parties
and play hostess*

EVERYONE, EVEN IF THEY ARE FAR TOO COOL to admit it, wants to be considered a fabulous host. Of course we want our friends to drool over our cooking and be amazed at our cocktail-making, but being a dazzling host is about more than whipping up a delicious feast or filling your flat with enough booze to keep a party swinging for the whole night (although these things often help). Most important is to throw the type of party that's right for you. If you hate cooking, then have a fun tea party and buy in all the cakes, or hire a barman and host a small cocktail party. This chapter will look at these kinds of occasion as well as more elaborate dinners.

Virtually every party guru will say the same thing when it comes to organizing any get-together, whether it's Sunday lunch for a few close friends or an elegant drinks party for thirty – it's all about the planning. Consummate hosts make entertaining look deceptively easy, but behind every successful gathering there has usually been a great deal of organization. They think very carefully about who to invite, as a good party is all about getting the mix right. And once the party is under way, good hosts make it look easy rather than scream when things go wrong or have a tantrum when their carpet gets ruined.

So while being the perfect host has a lot to do with making people feel at ease in your own home (which is no mean feat), it also has a lot to do with thinking about every detail and being prepared for any eventuality. But it's also important not to get too wrapped up in trying to get everything perfect; it should be fun to plan parties, deciding on the guest-list, choosing the menu, music, lights and décor. And as lovely as swanky bars and glamorous restaurants are, there's something cosy and intimate about entertaining in your home, and, best of all, at the end of the night you get to roll into bed rather than being tossed into the dark streets in search of a cab ride home.

Invitations

It is polite (not to mention considerate) to issue invitations a week or two in advance (for some busy people this could be a matter of months), and if you plan ahead it also means that you will be able to get the people you really want (even among friends everyone has a few firm party favourites). Also make sure that your guests know exactly when and where they are expected. It is much better to be thorough with instructions than have guests showing up at the wrong time or place.

Putting together the right mix of people is a great skill. Most of us have one or two jovial friends who are natural extroverts and seem to get along with anyone, and every good gathering needs at least one of these people. They are great at putting everyone else at ease. While you are dashing around in the kitchen or dealing with last-minute details, they become the perfect surrogate host, and for some strange reason they are usually adept at mixing drinks too (see Cocktails on page 213). Where possible, put together people who have some common interest or those you instinctively know will get on, and try to balance your guests so that there are some people who know each other and a few who do not, then everyone will be able to meet someone new.

Always think about the practicalities of your home. If you are giving a dinner, invite only the number of people who can comfortably fit around your dining table. While it might seem feasible to fit twelve people around a table for eight, trying to hold a conversation with a new acquaintance in a tight space is no fun. Old-school hosts insist on having even numbers of men and women around a table and seating them alternately, but don't get too hung up on rules. The main thing to consider is how well people will get on. You're not running some kind of dating agency around your kitchen table. These days some people seem to think it's cool to be late, but at dinner parties late-comers can be a nightmare and throw a cook completely out of kilter. Give late guests a reasonable amount of time to show up but don't feel bad about starting dinner without them if they are more than, say, an hour late. Especially if they haven't bothered to call and let you know where they are.

○ DO ask in advance if guests have any allergies, or, as is increasingly common, any special requirements. But don't feel obliged to pander endlessly to picky eating habits.

○ DO be specific about timings. If you want to serve dinner at 8.30p.m. then invite everyone for 8p.m. But do always allow some flexibility in your planning so that if someone is unavoidably detained it doesn't ruin the evening.

O DO give guests as much information and direction as possible if they haven't been to your place before. Strange areas can be confusing. Or refer them to *www.streetmap.co.uk*.

O DON'T invite guests at the last minute to fill in for someone else unless they are very good friends who will understand and be happy to help out.

O DON'T start drinking before guests arrive if you are a bit of a lightweight. If you have a lot to do in the kitchen, it's wise to start drinking only once the main course is on the table. Straining pans of boiling food is much harder in an alcoholic haze.

O DON'T try to build bridges between people you know dislike each other; they should be mixed only at bigger parties where they can avoid each other.

O DON'T stretch yourself too far. It is far better to have six people round for a relaxed supper than to try to create an elaborate dinner for ten and spend the evening feeling flustered and looking stressed.

First impressions

Being greeted by a serene and calm host in a welcoming home will instantly put your guests at ease, so try to make sure that you have most of the preparations done before people arrive.

Arriving at a dinner party and stumbling over a kitchen full of carrier bags, an unmade table and a cook on the verge of a domestic breakdown is unnerving for any guest.

Make sure that the outside of your home, including the path, and the entrance hall are tidy. Stepping over bin bags or tripping on jagged mats or piled-up shoes will not create a good first impression. (At worst you could find yourself wrapped up in a nasty lawsuit.) Also check that everything inside is as neat as possible and that there is a tidy bedroom or cloakroom where guests can drop off their coats or bags.

On a winter evening there is nothing like walking into a cosy, warm house bathed in soft candlelight. Softly lit rooms are calming and nurturing, and much more relaxing than harshly lit ones, so use lots of candles or dim the lights if possible – strong overhead lighting will kill any party. But don't burn scented candles during meals; their strong perfume will ruin the tastes and smells of the food.

O DO tidy your home a day or two before your party so that you have one less thing to worry about on the day.

O DO lay the table in the morning before leaving home if you have to go to work so you have less to do in the evening.

O DO make introductions efficiently as guests arrive, or get a friend to do it if you can't, so that no one is left stranded.

Tea parties

Tea has made a comeback in the past year or two and it's easy to see why. It doesn't take much planning to throw a tea party – just a little imagination – and they are a fun way to celebrate a baby shower, goddaughter's birthday or simply a gathering of friends. Aside from the tea, which should be made correctly (see overleaf), you should make delicate finger sandwiches. Scones, which should be light and fluffy, are traditional, but skipping them and getting straight to the cakes is acceptable, and if you don't have the time, talent or the inclination for baking, then buy the cakes in.

A few companies have cottoned on to the tea-party fixation and will deliver the prettiest cakes to your door. If you live in London or a big city, you will have lots of choice. **Coco London** (0870 7522590; *www.cocolondon.com*) delivers boxes of iced cakes to film premieres and glossy magazines such as *Vogue*; decorated with flowers or letters of your choice, they

TEA TIPS

from Bill Gorman,
Chairman of the Tea Council

BUY BEST quality tea. Good tea is hand picked and contains mostly young leaves, while cheaper tea has a high percentage of fibre.

ALWAYS BOIL freshly drawn water. Re-boiled water is deoxygenated and will give tea a metallic taste.

ALWAYS USE water that has fully boiled and allow the tea brewing time. Bags take less time to brew as the leaves are more finely cut. The time needed for loose-leaf tea depends on the delicacy of the brew.

MILK IN FIRST? Traditionally milk was poured in first to protect fine china cups from cracking. Later it was thought correct to pour the milk in first so the tea does not scald the fats in the milk. While many believe it is proper to pour the milk in last, there is no good reason to do so.

are perfect if you are celebrating something rather than just feasting on cakes for the sake of it. One of the best bakers in London is **Konditor and Cook** – their brownies are divine, and can be chopped up into inch-square bites (020 7261 0456). Notting Hill's most mouth-watering deli, **Ottolenghi**, has amazing tarts, cakes and huge meringues, all made on the premises (020 7727 1121). Elsewhere, visit traditional bakers and buy old-fashioned cakes such as éclairs and cream horns.

Even if your local supermarket is the only option, cakes such as Battenberg look pretty when sliced and even Mr Kipling's French fancies can look stunning piled up on top of a china cake stand. The right crockery is crucial – mismatched antique china is great although a full matching set of chintzy cups, saucers, plates and stands is elegant. Alternatively, stick to very simple bone china and the exquisite glass cake stands that are sold in their dozens in antiques shops.

○ DO serve sandwiches very slightly chilled, scones slightly warm and cakes at room temperature.

○ DO hunt for gorgeous vintage cake forks with colourful handles and other cutlery at antiques fairs – they look beautiful at teatime.

○ DON'T leave sandwiches uncovered as they will dehydrate in no time at all. Keep them covered with a damp tea towel somewhere cool.

○ DO (if you are a bit of a Channel hopper) plan ahead and organize your tea party for the day after a trip to Paris – go to **Ladurée** in the Madeleine and stock up on its divine candy-coloured miniature macaroons. It even does seasonal colours, including macaroons covered in gold leaf at Christmas.

Cocktail parties

Cocktail parties are utterly glamorous. They are the perfect excuse to make exotic drinks and get dolled up in a cocktail dress and piles of sparkling jewels. Traditionally held from around 6.30p.m. until 8.30p.m., cocktail parties would end as guests left for later dinner engagements, but these days they are more often thrown as the main entertainment rather than a side show, and roll on until well past supper-time. It is easy to assume that the more people you invite the more lively your party will be, but it's not necessarily so, and as a cocktail party should be a kind of fun yet elegant gathering, smaller numbers, say around twenty people, are probably about right. If you invite more than this, you will need to have a barman too; mixing countless cocktails by yourself will quickly lose its novelty. Anyway, there is nothing quite so chic as a handsome barman shaking cocktails in your home. If you don't want to have the expense of a professional barman, you could persuade a suitably savvy friend to take up the role.

○ DO plan music and lighting ahead of time. Both are crucial to creating the right environment.

○ DON'T clear away all the furniture – there should be areas where people can sit as well as areas where small groups can stand and chat.

○ DO provide something more substantial than a bowl of nuts – plates of antipasti and bowls of roughly cut chunks of Parmesan are both delicious and filling.

○ DO make sure that bathrooms are well stocked with loo paper, soap and clean towels.

○ DO make sure there is plenty of ventilation – rooms quickly overheat with a boozy crowd. Always open some windows to allow fresh air to circulate.

○ DON'T lecture guests about smoking or banish them outside. If you are throwing a party, you have to accept that some people may want to smoke. Leave ashtrays around the rooms and remember to empty them often.

Cocktails from the Savoy

The Savoy's American Bar has played host to stars from Marlene Dietrich and Fred and Ginger to Sean Connery and Frank Sinatra (who used to relax after concerts by playing the piano here). Harry Craddock, the bar's famous head barman and author of *The Savoy Cocktail Book*, introduced the Martini to Britain. Salim Khoury, who has worked at the Savoy since 1969, is currently head barman; here he supplies some classic cocktail recipes.

Champagne Cocktail

$^8/_{10}$ Champagne
$^2/_{10}$ cognac
sugar cube
Angostura bitters

Put a sugar cube into a chilled Champagne glass and douse with a few drops of bitters; allow the bitters to soak in. Pour over the cognac and then fill the glass with champagne. Decorate with a sliver of orange peel.

Cosmopolitan

$^{3}/_{10}$ vodka
$^{3}/_{10}$ cranberry juice
$^{2}/_{10}$ triple sec or Cointreau
$^{2}/_{10}$ fresh lime juice

Shake all the ingredients together with ice. Strain and pour into a chilled cocktail glass and decorate with a slice of lime on the side of the glass.

Manhattan

$^{7}/_{10}$ rye whisky
$^{3}/_{10}$ sweet Martini
Angostura bitters

Mix the whisky and the Martini over ice, add a dash of Angostura bitters and stir well. Pour into a chilled cocktail glass and decorate with a cherry.

Margarita

$^{4}/_{10}$ Tequila
$^{3}/_{10}$ Cointreau or triple sec
$^{3}/_{10}$ lime juice
splash sugar syrup
splash egg white

Dip the rim of a chilled Margarita glass in lemon juice then in salt. Mix all the ingredients together, shake well and pour into the glass.

Martini

9/10 gin
1/10 extra dry vermouth

Fill a glass jar with ice. Pour over the gin and add the vermouth. Stir well, then strain into a chilled Martini glass. Garnish with a sliver of lemon peel or a green olive.

Mojito

freshly chopped lime and mint leaves
2/10 sugar
6/10 white rum
2/10 fresh lime juice

Put a small handful of freshly chopped lime and a small handful of mint leaves into a chilled tumbler with some sugar and crush well. Pour over the white rum and lime juice and fill the glass with crushed ice.

Racing Lady

$^3/_{10}$ gin
$^3/_{10}$ Grand Marnier
$^2/_{10}$ lime juice
$^2/_{10}$ Champagne

Wet the rim of a chilled cocktail glass with a piece of lemon and dip it into caster sugar. Shake the gin, Grand Marnier and lime juice together well. Pour into the glass and top up with Champagne. Decorate with a Cape gooseberry.

Savoy Royale

chopped fresh strawberries and white peach
$^2/_{10}$ strawberry liqueur
$^2/_{10}$ peach liqueur
$^6/_{10}$ Champagne

Mash a few strawberries with the strawberry liqueur and put into a chilled glass. Mash a little chopped white peach with peach liqueur and add to the glass. Top up with Champagne.

Whisky Sour

$^4/_{10}$ rye whisky
$^3/_{10}$ lemon juice
$^3/_{10}$ sugar syrup
splash egg white

Mix all the ingredients together and shake well. Pour into a short chilled glass and decorate with a small sliver of orange peel and a cherry.

COCKTAIL-MAKING TIPS
from Salim Khoury,
head barman at the Savoy

ALWAYS use well-chilled glasses for cocktails. (Leave them to stand for a few minutes with ice inside if they are not cool enough or you don't have enough room in your freezer to chill them.)

DON'T over-decorate – simple garnishes look best.

AS A GENERAL RULE, opaque cocktails are shaken while clear cocktails are stirred.

SHAKEN COCKTAILS should be well shaken, with vigorous movements to mix the ingredients well.

NEVER re-use ice.

GIN should always be used from the freezer as it will not freeze; vodka can be stored in the freezer, too.

White Lady

$^4/_{10}$ gin
$^3/_{10}$ Cointreau or triple sec
$^3/_{10}$ lemon juice

Mix the gin, Cointreau and lemon juice over ice. Shake well.
Pour into a chilled cocktail glass and decorate with a cherry.

Canapés

Canapés, whether hot, cold or a mixture of both, are essential
at a cocktail party – a bowl of crisps is not substantial enough.
But there is an art to serving the right kind of canapé. They
need to be easy to eat and this means making everything bite-
size – it is tricky to hold a conversation, clutch a glass and try
to eat a messy, oversized canapé or one that falls apart as soon
as it is lifted from the plate. Anything that will potentially drip
is not a good idea – you don't want to be held responsible for
destroying your friend's brand-new Missoni sweater. The time
of year is also important, not only in terms of the kind of food
you should serve but also what will be in season. On a balmy
summer evening, light, fresh foods are appropriate – asparagus tips with a fresh aioli mayonnaise, figs wrapped in Parma
ham or cherry tomatoes wrapped in a basil leaf are all light
and summery. In autumn and winter, canapés should be more
warming and hearty. Espresso cups filled with a delicious
home-made soup are easy both to prepare and to serve.
Gordon Ramsay serves appetizers this way: frothy soups driz-
zled with truffle oil. And this is a great way to finally use a

collection of espresso cups that has been gathering dust in the cupboard.

Serving canapés before dinner is sometimes appropriate too. Don't assume that guests can happily wait for some time to eat – if they have come straight from work, they are probably hungry. Having something ready to serve before dinner, even if it's only a big bowl of warmed almonds or other nuts, will also give you more time to finish things in the kitchen. If you are going to make appetizers, then it's important that they fit with whatever you will be serving, and shouldn't be so filling as to spoil everyone's appetite.

○ DO buy food in for a cocktail party if you don't have time to prepare it. Canapés are the most fiddly and time-consuming of things to make. Boxes of sushi are perfect, and look great too.

DINNER PARTY BOOKS

TO KEEP TRACK of what you have cooked and for whom, buy a notebook and keep a record of your dinner parties. **Smythson** sell notebooks designed for this by mail order: 020 7318 1515, but obviously any notebook will do. Make a list of who came as well as what food was served and which wines, and your honest verdict of what was well received. It will prove a useful aid, and will ensure that you don't cook the same thing for the same people.

○ DO allow five or six canapés per person for pre-dinner, and up to sixteen for a cocktail party.

○ DO consider serving more substantial appetizers at a dinner party instead of a starter. This will give you more time in the kitchen and make cooking less stressful.

○ DON'T become obsessed with what is fashionable – stick to classics that are always popular, such as smoked salmon and blinis, cheese straws, oysters, hot cocktail sausages.

○ DO keep it simple – as with all cooking, the best ingredients served as naturally as possible always work best.

Planning a dinner party

What you serve depends on many different things, but primarily on how good a cook you are (be realistic here) and how calm and organized you are when cooking for more than a few people. When you plan a menu, avoid doing more than one tricky or work-intensive course – you don't want to spend the whole evening running around the kitchen while your guests are all at the table. That's no fun for you or for them. There are certain things to steer clear of if you are cooking for a multitude. Risottos are probably best left for kitchen suppers with a few friends because you have to be at the pan stirring religiously during cooking. Recipes that require pan-frying or char-grilling also become quite complicated when cooking for larger numbers because the kitchen gets smoky and you have to juggle plates to keep everything hot.

Make sure your menu is balanced. It sounds obvious, but you might forget while you enthusiastically browse cookbooks. If your first course is very rich, choose a light main course. For example, if you are serving foie gras as a starter, don't follow it with beef Wellington. Think about textures and flavours. Don't serve soup as a starter with stew as a main course or your friends might feel as though they are eating at a retirement home. Similarly, don't repeat the same foods in different courses; don't start with a tomato tart, say, then use tomatoes as a side dish for the main course. By pudding time you might not feel like attempting anything challenging. Keep things simple, or prepare in advance, or buy something special. Tarts with a dollop of crème fraiche or cream are always a treat, but so too are the simplest things. Fresh fruit in season is always good at the end of a meal. Or skip pudding altogether and do a cheese course.

○ DO cook in one pot. A stew, pie, pot roast or anything else that can happily cook away in the oven cuts down time slaving in the kitchen.

○ DO limit complex work in the final stages to the starter – guests can be chatting over drinks while you prepare the food. But if your main course is unavoidably labour-intensive, then consider an easy starter: plates of antipasti, for example, or a substantial salad, or even soup, which can always be prepared ahead (even by a few days) and then left to simmer gently on its own, causing no trouble at all.

○ DO give your guests a chance to relax during courses, but don't leave very long gaps between – about fifteen minutes is perfect.

○ DON'T skimp – if you can't afford to spend lots of money, plan an economical meal with cheaper ingredients that you can buy in generous quantities. There's nothing worse than not having enough of everything.

○ DON'T ever attempt more than one course that you haven't cooked before.

○ DO buy a course to save on time and effort, such as a patisserie-made tart for pudding.

○ DO clear plates away quickly, but don't stack them at the table.

Table settings

If a beautifully laid table is one of the first things your guests see, it will make them infinitely more excited about dinner,

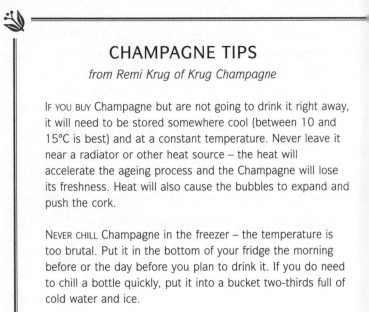

CHAMPAGNE TIPS

from Remi Krug of Krug Champagne

IF YOU BUY Champagne but are not going to drink it right away, it will need to be stored somewhere cool (between 10 and 15°C is best) and at a constant temperature. Never leave it near a radiator or other heat source – the heat will accelerate the ageing process and the Champagne will lose its freshness. Heat will also cause the bubbles to expand and push the cork.

NEVER CHILL Champagne in the freezer – the temperature is too brutal. Put it in the bottom of your fridge the morning before or the day before you plan to drink it. If you do need to chill a bottle quickly, put it into a bucket two-thirds full of cold water and ice.

tea, brunch or whatever else you are serving. This does not mean a stiff and formal affair with a towering floral arrangement and crisply starched linens (although antique linens are lovely), simply that your table should look organized and welcoming. Even if you have just invited a few friends round for a gossipy weekend lunch, an inviting table will set a calm and cosseting tone.

Don't feel you have to have a centrepiece, which can look old-fashioned, and anyway hinders cross-table debate; talking

BEFORE OPENING the bottle always think about which way it is pointing – avoid aiming it at fine china, a precious painting, the chandeliers or an aged relative.

ALWAYS TURN the bottle with one hand and keep your other hand at the top with your fingers over the cork – this gives you more control.

TULIP-SHAPED glasses or flutes are the best for champagne. Coupes, which became popular in the 1920s, not only let the bubbles evaporate but also allow the aroma of the champagne to disappear quickly.

CHAMPAGNE can be re-corked with a champagne stopper. It should be fine the next day, although it may have lost a little fizz.

through a vast structure of delphiniums and peonies might be amusing but eye-to-eye contact with other guests is preferable. Whether you use a tablecloth depends a great deal on how good your table is or how much you want to protect it from spilled wine or food. For a more formal dinner, however, a perfectly laundered and pressed cloth can transform a mediocre table into a beautiful one. A crumpled, creased, tatty old tablecloth will not look elegant at all. Cloth napkins are a wise investment if you plan to hold lots of dinner parties.

Paper ones are fine for casual meals with old friends, but proper napkins are nicer to use and simply look and work better; a set of good quality ones should give years of service. Try to keep place settings symmetrical. That is not to say that you must whip out a ruler like a country-house butler and with *Gosford Park*-style efficiency measure each setting to the millimetre, but do make sure that places are evenly spaced and reasonably uniform and neat.

How much crockery, cutlery and glass you put out depends on what you are serving, but it's worth remembering that the more you have on the table, the less you will need to get up and fetch during the meal. All cutlery should be arranged starting from the outside and working in, with knives on the right (with blades facing inwards) and forks on the left, unless there is a course that requires a fork alone, in which case it sits on the right-hand side. Put out water glasses as well as wine glasses – to the top right of each place setting. And have plates for other courses stacked in a convenient place so they are close to hand when you need them.

On the subject of plates, if you are going to entertain regularly, it is worth investing in some good china. Plain white is classical and practical. If you want to economize, hunt out shops that sell surplus or discontinued stock from top makers such as Wedgwood and Thomas Goode. One of the best ones is **Pot Luck** in Columbia Road, in east London. The shop sells immaculate china and it is possible to put together a vast dinner service on a shoestring here (020 7722 6892).

The main course should be served at the table. In the wake of endless cookery programmes, home cooks now tend to spend ages in the kitchen labouring over mini-towers of food immaculately dressed in an artwork of sauces. Serving the main course at the table is generally much easier and a lot less pretentious. If something is simpler to dish up in the kitchen, such as a messy stew, or a delicate recipe you would rather serve yourself away from your guests, you can still put the accompanying vegetables or whatever else in big bowls and let people help themselves to these at the table. Ultimately, though, do whatever works for you – a happy cook makes for happy guests.

○ DO keep your table neutral and relaxing. Crazy colour schemes can be too glitzy and off-putting. As with crockery, simple and neutral is safest.

○ DON'T fill the table so that there's no sense of space; guests shouldn't feel that there's no room to spread out or they are too close to their neighbours.

○ DO use candles to create a cosy atmosphere, but don't use scented candles when serving food.

○ DON'T fill wine glasses to the top. They should be half or just over half full.

○ DO encourage everyone to help themselves to wine, unless you want to spend the evening as sommelier.

○ DO make sure that cutlery is spotlessly clean and shiny. Rewash it if it hasn't been used for a while to make it gleam. Ditto glasses.

○ DON'T even think about creating an origami masterpiece with the napkins. Fold them neatly into rectangles and leave them either on serving dishes or to the left of the forks.

○ DO warm dishes for hot courses to prevent your food from cooling too quickly.

Serving wine with food

Think about how flavoursome the food is and match it with the depth of flavour in the wine. So put hearty foods such as stews and casseroles with full-bodied reds, and more subtly flavoured food with lighter wine. Ignore the rules about chicken and fish being served with white wine and red meat with red. Instead think about the whole dish – if a chicken is served in a rich buttery sauce it might be better suited to a red Burgundy than a white wine.

If you are taking a bottle to a dinner party and don't know what's on the menu, go for lighter wines such as Chablis, Muscadet or a delicate Riesling, or light reds such as Valpolicella or a young, fruity Pinot Noir. Similarly, if you are catering for a party choose lighter wines such as Sancerre, Sauvignon Blanc, Beaujolais and Valpolicella. Allow half a bottle of red per person and a little more for white. In summer, trade Champagne for a more economical bubbly such as Prosecco or Cava, and allow half a bottle per person.

Wine partners

Beef Dense reds such as Cabernet Sauvignon, Bordeaux and Barolo go well with roast beef; spicier reds such as Shiraz, Grenache and Amarone are all good partners for hearty stews.

Lamb Red Bordeaux or Merlot are good overall choices, but for lighter lamb dishes choose a young Pinot Noir. If you are serving offal, partner it with a Barolo.

Pork Beaujolais goes brilliantly with roast pork and cassoulet, although more full-bodied reds such as Shiraz mix well with sausages, while Chablis is a good choice for cooked ham.

Chicken Roast chicken can be served with Chardonnay or a white Bordeaux, but for heartier stews choose a light Italian red such as Chianti or a Merlot.

Game Pinot Noir, red Burgundy and Merlot are all good matches for game, although fuller-flavoured game dishes such as stews would be best with a full-bodied red such as Cabernet Sauvignon. More delicate game can be served with a lighter red, such as a Côtes du Rhône. For pheasant, try a dry Pinot Gris.

WINE TIPS

from Simon Berry, of Berry Bros and Rudd

It's fun to know lots about wine but it's not crucial. There are enough people around whose job it is to know all about the subject, so buy wine from a wine merchant who can give you thorough and expert advice on which wines are best for your needs.

If you can't get to a specialist, or are embarrassed to go into a shop where you can't pronounce the names let alone make a choice, then buy on the internet. On the **Berry Bros** site *(www.bbr.com)* there is a pronunciation guide so you can learn how to say the names of producers for when you do want to buy in person.

The basic, although breakable, rules of serving wine with food are as follows: serve light wine before heavier wine; white before red; dry before sweet; young before old.

If you take wine to a dinner party, don't be upset if it isn't opened – your host has probably chosen wine and food for the occasion. If you are the host, don't feel you have to open wine that people have brought with them.

Fish Delicate dishes should be served with light whites such as Sancerre, Pinot Grigio and Muscadet, while richer-sauced fish would work well with white Burgundy. Oily fish such as mackerel is good with Muscadet or Sancerre, and meatier fish such as salmon and tuna are best with a Chardonnay. Smoked salmon, oysters and lobster all have a natural (and costly) affinity with Champagne.

Salads Vinegar-based dressings make salads hard to match with wine but try light rosés or citrusy whites such as Sancerre and Pinot Grigio.

Puddings Always serve wines that are sweeter than the food. For rich chocolatey puddings and fruitcakes try a Madeira, and for light fruit or creamy puddings an Orange Muscat or Sauternes.

Drinks

Dealing with drink orders when you are up to your elbows in steaming pots in the kitchen can be stressful. By far the best way to deal with this is to get someone else to do it for you. Nominate a friend to oversee the drinks, and perhaps even ask him or her to greet your guests. Make sure it's someone friendly who won't scare the other guests. There's usually one charismatic person who enjoys being given the chance to work the room and get to know anyone they haven't met before.

Keeping the drinks to a few simple choices makes matters easier for everyone. If you give guests too many options, they could feel awkward about making a decision and it will take much longer to serve the drinks. In winter, it is always nice to be offered something warming, such as a Champagne cocktail or a whisky sour. In summer, make up big jugs of a refreshing cocktail such as Mojito; pouring from a jug saves making up each drink individually and so is less time-consuming. Have the glasses, bottles and ice ready, and preferably away from where you are preparing the food if you can.

☆ ☆ ☆ ☆ ☆ ☆ ☆ ☆ ☆ ☆ ☆

CHOCOLATES

Even after a rich pudding it's always good to serve something sweet with coffee, and of course some really good chocolates could replace pudding altogether. Quality chocolate with a high cocoa count is perfect to serve with coffee, and anything from the shops below (or other good producers) will be top notch. However, cheaper chocolate can provoke just as much excitement. Fill a gorgeous glass bowl with sweets such as Maltesers or Smarties, or mix up a selection of miniature chocolate bars and chopped-up chunks from normal-sized bars.

L'Artisan du Chocolat (020 7824 8365) is a young London-based company that makes really original ganaches, available via mail order, which are flavoured with everything

☆ ☆ ☆ ☆ ☆ ☆ ☆ ☆ ☆ ☆ ☆

There's nothing worse than dealing with a culinary crisis when you have a gaggle of onlookers.

While most guests will turn up with a bottle of something, never rely on people arriving with wine for dinner. Always have more than enough bottles to avoid an emergency sprint to the off-licence, which is never very elegant and will interrupt your evening. Having as much in as anyone could conceivably want will certainly make for a better party.

☆ ☆ ☆ ☆ ☆ ☆ ☆ ☆ ☆ ☆ ☆ ☆

from Earl Grey or lapsang souchong to lavender and tobacco. The salted caramels are pretty incredible, too.

Truffles piled on a cake stand or a pretty bonbon dish look great. Order from the Chocolate Society, which began as an importer of Valrhona chocolate and now sells a whole range of chocolates from its London shop and via mail order (01423 322238).

Pierre Marcolini (020 7795 6611) is the place to go for seriously fabulous chocolates. Everything is made with chocolate containing from 60 to 80 per cent cocoa solids, which gives the results a deep, decadent flavour. These are truly sublime – and the pralines are utterly, mouth-wateringly scrumptious.

☆ ☆ ☆ ☆ ☆ ☆ ☆ ☆ ☆ ☆ ☆

Whatever you personally prefer to drink, don't narrow the choice too much – not everyone will share your passion for organic raspberry wine. However carefully you have selected wines, it is considerate also to have something else to offer guests. Remember that not everyone will be drinking alcohol – some may be driving, or simply not want to drink. Don't force non-drinkers to have a drink, and try to have something

TIPS ON ENTERTAINING ITALIAN-STYLE

from Giorgio Armani

JUST BEFORE DINNER, I like to play a compilation of ethnic underground music because I think it creates a relaxing atmosphere. As the evening continues, I like to change the music to more of a beat, which can range from soul to R&B. If it becomes a party, then I play compilations of dance and hip-hop.

THERE IS NOTHING WORSE than a dinner that is trying too hard – whether it is because there are too many sauces, butter, garlic or cream, or just too many ingredients in the wrong combinations. When I am entertaining, I stick to a simple menu rich in quality and natural ingredients, such as pasta with fresh tomato sauce, fresh vegetables, simple meat and fish dishes that are dressed with purest olive oil, lemon or on hand besides water and the ubiquitous orange juice, such as elderflower pressé or fresh lemonade.

○ DO invest in a set of flutes and large wine glasses – matching glasses make a table look much neater, and you don't want to spoil good Champagne or wine with ugly glasses.

---

fresh herbs. Simple courses with natural ingredients are not only the most enjoyed and appreciated meals, but also considered the most elegant and chic.

I THINK BOTH fragrance and flowers are important to a cocktail party. Fragrance has to be simple and understated [Armani parties are famous for being filled with Diptyque's Fig scent]. I love using incense because it creates a sense of mystery without being too heavy. This goes for the choice of flowers as well. Simple is the best solution, because flowers should be an accompanying element, not an attention-grabbing centrepiece.

KEEP EVERYTHING SIMPLE and relaxed. Last summer, I finished my new boat Mariú and spent every possible free moment on it and was constantly entertaining. Living on a boat, everyone goes barefoot in a sarong the whole time – a relaxed natural ambience but this does not mean that one has to forfeit luxury.

○ DO fill the freezer with ice – it's easy to forget, but you will not be able to mix drinks without it, and it's handy for chilling wine quickly.

○ DON'T use nasty plastic glasses. If you are having a party and don't have enough glasses, hire more. Majestic and other drinks companies hire out any number of glasses for free.

○ DON'T serve wine in dark coloured glasses; lightly coloured antique glasses, however, can look pretty.

Coffee

Serving coffee or after-dinner drinks is something of a ritual and can act as a grand finale – a sort of final flourish just when your guests think all the fun is over. It's also an opportunity (as if you need another one) to impress your friends with your innate stylishness. Prepare a tray before dinner so you simply have to boil a kettle when the time comes; after an evening of cooking and several glasses of wine, even the simplest tasks can become a struggle. Invest in some excellent, freshly ground coffee and always have some herbal teas for non-coffee drinkers.

○ DO serve coffee on an interesting old tray. It's easy to pick these up second-hand. You could even use a retro trolley, which has an ironic Fifties-hostess air about it.

○ DO serve coffee in pretty, mismatched cups and saucers from antiques shops and markets – they look delicate and quirky.

○ DO use colourful little demitasse spoons, which are also easy to find at antiques shops and markets.

Parting thoughts

It is, of course, a tribute to your supreme hospitality, but some guests can be particularly thick-skinned when it comes to knowing when to leave a party. Conversely, stroppy hosts who suddenly decide they are tired or have had enough can ruin a happy evening by ejecting their guests in an unceremonious fashion. One high-profile New York hostess has even been known to flick the light switches on and off when she wants her guests to go home. Subtler measures are just as effective – and are a lot more polite.

If yawning or clearing up does-n't work, offer guests a bed for the night. This is the politest way to hint without causing any offence that you are ready to go to sleep. Always make sure you have the telephone numbers of local taxi firms to hand – if they are a reliable firm you have used in the past, so much the better.

Etiquette

A modern guide to manners and model behaviour

SOCIAL GRACES ARE AS RELEVANT now as they have ever been, but it sometimes seems impossible to keep up with the ever-changing codes. We live in an age when most men don't know whether a woman will find it thoughtful or patronizing if he opens the door for her. It's a time when jeans are deemed acceptable for the smartest parties yet strictly off-limits in some hotel bars. It's not surprising that we all get a bit confused – it's a social minefield out there.

Knowing how to do the right thing, during day-to-day routines or at formal occasions, will make life much, much easier. It is hard for anyone to avoid completely the occasions in life for which the correct form still stands, and at some point we all have to go to parties, weddings and christenings, but if you know what is expected of you it's much easier to relax and have fun, and, as a guest at any function, having a good time without embarrassing yourself is surely the whole point.

Hosting a house party

House parties should be a bit like sleepovers but with better conversation and, hopefully, much better food. While the most important consideration is that everyone has fun, there are lots of things to think about before inviting friends to stay in your home, whether it is for one night or a long weekend. If a close friend is staying then everything should be pretty straightforward – all you have to do is provide warm hospitality and a comfortable bed – but when a few people are involved, who might not know each other, it becomes a little more complicated.

Whether you are inviting by phone or more formally in a letter, try to plan well in advance, especially over the summer months and holidays, when everyone's weekends tend to get booked up quickly. If you are inviting a few people, then think carefully about the mix, as it's crucial, or at least preferable, that everyone gets on well. Always let them know when they are expected to arrive (and leave), send some maps and transport details if they are travelling far and have never visited before, and if you have special activities planned then let them know in advance. There's little point in organizing an afternoon of tennis if your guests have only bought slinky Jimmy Choos and cocktail dresses.

Bedrooms or sleeping areas should be well organized, cosy and well aired. A comfortable bed with freshly laundered sheets and fluffy towels (small and large) are essential. As a guide, think about whether you would like to sleep there, and if the answer is no, you shouldn't expect your friends to sleep there either. Make sure there's a bedside lamp, as well as some water and a glass and something delicious to nibble on in case of night-time hunger pangs. Put some fresh garden flowers in the room to brighten it up (or buy a couple of stems of something fragrant like lily of the valley, which will smell delicious) or burn a lovely candle so the room feels more lived in. Leave something good to read, whether it's a pile of the latest magazines, which are always welcome reading, or some books you know they will enjoy.

When your guests arrive, give them a chance to sort themselves out, unpack and have a bath; it's horrible arriving somewhere after a long journey and being whisked out for the evening feeling crumpled and unwashed. Explain where everything is so they can help themselves throughout their stay and feel more at home, and let them know what you have planned for the weekend, bearing in mind that everyone will probably welcome some free time. Activities can be fun, but everyone appreciates some relaxing down-time.

○ DO try to have everything organized ahead of time so you don't have to run around doing last-minute shopping. Have a good selection of things for breakfast, and bear in mind that your guests might want things that you would not usually buy. Having friends to stay is also the perfect excuse for the proper breakfast there's usually no time for.

○ DO tell guests about your home's idiosyncrasies. If hot water is in short supply or you have temperamental plumbing, let guests know when they arrive.

○ DO plan the weekend to a degree, but don't have a strict routine that must be adhered to unless you want your friends to feel as though they have stumbled into a girl-guide adventure. Allow some time for them to do things on their own too.

○ DON'T forget to leave some extra pillows and a blanket in bedrooms, especially if your house has biting Arctic chills.

TIPS ON BEING
THE PERFECT HOST...

from Theo Fennell

THE PERFECT HOST puts you so at ease that you do all the work yourself. This is the state I try to achieve. Encourage guests to pour their own drinks, get logs and not complain too much at the plainness of one's food and the monstrous quality of one's wine.

PUT A TELEVISION, drinks tray and a really good selection of arcane books (with plenty of bizarre pictures) in the bedrooms so people can disappear and not clutter downstairs before dinner, or indeed ever.

TRY TO KEEP dinners in-house. If you pad out with the locals they need to be very amusing indeed. The local solicitor teamed with a media power couple from London is disastrous.

MAKE SURE no one misses anything they want to see on television, such as sports, final episodes, or themselves. It's easy to check, and if you are the cause of their loss, the sulk will be phenomenal and forgiveness unlikely.

Being a guest

The ideal guest is easy to spot – they are the ones who are invited often, and their plus points are not so different from those of a good host. They are thoughtful (they turn up on time and arrive with welcome goodies), easy-going (they don't have tantrums when they lose every game of Scrabble) and good company and fun to be with. Spending a weekend away can be brilliant fun or a social nightmare, depending on what you expect and how well prepared you are. Obviously it depends on who you are staying with. If you are visiting a close friend, and spending an evening feasting on sweets and watching chick flicks, you have little to worry about. If, on the other hand, you are a guest of aged friends, distant relatives or terrifying in-laws whom you barely know or like, then you need some psychological preparation.

Although you are a guest you shouldn't expect everything to be done for you, so find out where things are so that you can help yourself. Even if you feel a bit awkward poking around someone else's kitchen cupboards, your hosts will probably want you to feel that you can make yourself a cup of coffee. If you wake up early in the morning then quietly make a drink and entertain yourself. Early risers should not be seen or heard.

Take an active part in whatever your hosts have planned for the weekend but don't feel that you must take part in every activity, and if you don't want to reveal yourself in a swimsuit then simply say so. You shouldn't feel bullied into doing anything you don't want to. Similarly, don't expect to visit friends for the weekend and collapse on the sofa for forty-eight hours; as a guest you should sing for your supper, or at least try to.

○ DO call ahead and let your host know if you are going to be late. Ruining the supper on your first night will not set a good tone for the rest of your stay. Similarly, try not to turn up hours early either, as this is just as disruptive.

○ DO arrive with a gift – flowers, good chocolates and Champagne are always a welcome treat, but if you know the host well then try to think of something more personal (see opposite).

○ DO try to be nice to other house guests (even if you don't like them very much).

○ DO try to keep your bedroom and bathroom tidy; your host shouldn't have to spend the weekend acting as your chambermaid. This is their home, not a hotel.

○ DO offer to help with chores such as washing-up or shopping, but once your offer has been refused, do not insist. Territorial hosts might not want a helping hand.

○ DO always send a thank-you note to your host.

○ DON'T leave things behind. It's a pain for your
host to have to post forgotten items, and quite
embarrassing for you to have left your knickers
under someone else's bed, so always check your
room before you leave.

○ DON'T outstay your welcome. If you have agreed
to leave after lunch on Sunday, don't hang around
just because you are having such a good time.
As much as your friends love your company,
they might have other plans for the rest of their
weekend.

The house-gift

Buying a house-gift can throw even the most knowledgeable
shopper into a panic. If your hosts are wealthy, stylish, or
even mind-blowingly dull, it's trickier still. The gift has to be
substantial enough to show that you are grateful for the invitation, but at the same time you don't want to blow a major
proportion of your income on a token gesture. Consider who
you will be staying with and try to think what they would like,
rather than taking the most predictable gift. No one is going
to be dismissive of some gorgeous chocolates, Champagne
(always welcome to me) or fabulous wine, but there are far
more imaginative presents. The secret, or at least one of the
secrets, of good gift-giving is to think laterally and be inven-
tive. Having a stockpile of gifts in readiness is a good idea,
unless you like to find something very specific for each person

– this way you can buy lovely presents when you see them and keep them for when you need them. For some reason we can all think of great gifts when there's no pressure, but as soon as we absolutely need to find something it's impossible to find anything at all.

○ DO take care when recycling a gift. If you must do it, remember who gave it to you in the first place.

○ DO remember that presentation is everything. Put the gift in a nice bag and pad it with some crumpled tissue paper, but there is no need to wrap house-gifts.

○ DO, if you are feeling generous, send flowers after the weekend. If ordering them through a local florist, be specific about what you want – if you don't know your florist's style, play it safe by asking them to send one type of flower, such as one fat bunch of hyacinths, anemones or roses. You can even post a card to the florist to be delivered with the flowers.

For sleepovers and weekends with girlfriends

Make a 'girls night in' hamper packed with indulgent treats for the weekend, such as face masks, scrubs, boxes of highly calorific chocolates, candles and DVDs.

TIPS ON BEING
THE PERFECT GUEST

from Christian Louboutin

IF YOU ARE STAYING in a house you have never been invited to before, and if you fly to get there, always stop by the airport lounge to fill your pockets with as many crackers, crisps, biscuits or peanuts as you can. One never knows; these might come in handy if you are starving in the middle of the night.

IF A LONG DRIVE is organized with a party of more than two, steer clear of large bottles of water. Stopping every half hour for your convenience will drive everybody crazy, including yourself.

A GOOD GUEST should never expect to be welcome in someone's house for more than three days. On the day of arrival, it is essential to provide an excuse why you will have to leave after your third night. That way, everybody will be at ease. If you are invited to stay for longer, it will be a great surprise; if you aren't, it will just be as planned. Perfect.

I PREFER SENDING out a lovely photo album of the weekend as a thank-you, long after it would be expected (a minimum of two months after your stay). It always makes for a wonderful surprise.

Give things in beautiful packaging. Packs of soap, lovely bath oils and any other toiletries in pretty printed wrapping are always a winner, and a girl can never have too many luxurious bath products. **Santa Maria Novella** in Walton Street, London SW3 make the most delectable toiletries known to man and they are available by mail order (020 7460 6600) – you don't need to spend a fortune, just a couple of lovely soaps is a treat.

Scented candles, especially if they are from Diptyque, Votivo or L'Artisan Parfumeur, are a failsafe thing to give to girls.

For country weekends with groups of friends

Order some DVDs or videos from *www.amazon.co.uk*. This is a great idea if you are staying in a remote house and the weather forecast is hideous. Take bags of sticky popcorn and cheap pick-and-mix sweets too. Think about who is in the group and cater the films to them.

If it is autumn or winter, a cosy blanket is a lovely gift. Stick to neutral colours and buy the best quality you can afford.

Summer rentals

A stack of the summer's best books is something everyone can use and will also provide talking points when you are all bored of each other's conversation. Add some classics, too, for guests who have already read all the bestsellers.

A good game that brings out a competitive streak in your more timid friends is also a fun house-gift and, as above, will provide entertainment for evenings in.

Put together a cocktail kit with plenty of spirits and every-thing else needed to make your chosen cocktail.

Grand and slightly intimidating older hosts

Put together a box of foodie treats appropriate to the people you are staying with. Really good olive oil, vinegar and Parmesan would go down a storm with cosmopolitan hosts, while reclusive aged relatives would probably love whisky, bis-cuits and yummy chocolates.

For keen gardeners, order something from **RK Alliston** (0845 130 5577), who have a mail-order catalogue packed with chic and useful gardening kit. Or, rather than taking flowers, which can be a bother to arrange in the whirl of guests arriving at a house, buy a beautifully scented rose bush.

Antique linens are a special gift. Sets of napkins or pillowcases are easy to find in antiques shops and markets. Pack them up with some lavender bags, too.

Dinner party form

Being invited to eat with friends is a joy. To begin with, some-one else has done all the work, which is a big relief, or at least it should be. They will also be doing the clearing up, which is even better. There's a primal element to this too: eating with others is a fundamental part of our social lives, and it's impor-tant to remember that while you are being entertained, you still have an important role to play, and your part is almost as crucial as your host's. If you are eating with good friends then you will probably feel totally at ease. If, on the other hand, you have been invited by your new boss or friends you have only just met, there are suddenly a few more stumbling blocks.

Whether you are having supper with old friends, a big Sunday lunch with distant family or a more formal dinner, you should dress up a bit for the occasion, even if all that means is looking a bit more groomed than usual. Someone has cared enough to cook for you so you should show that you have made an effort, though this doesn't mean whipping out a taffeta ballgown for a dinner party.

Unless you are in a situation where you know everyone, you will probably be meeting new people, and if for some reason you haven't been introduced, then simply introduce yourself. Try to talk to everyone around you; even if the person on one side of you happens to be endlessly entertaining, you should always make an effort to talk to the person on your other side too. We are all guilty of spending evenings chatting to one person we already know rather than meeting anyone new.

What to take

In some circles there is still the stuffy assumption that it's bad form to take wine to a dinner party – as though it implies that the host doesn't have good enough wine of his own. Of course, few of us are lucky enough to have a brilliantly stocked cellar, and most of us are happy to give, and receive, wine. Choosing what to take can be pretty daunting, especially if your hosts are wine buffs. The best way around this is to buy decent wine from a good wine merchant, and if you are visiting a connoisseur, then choose something a bit unusual. Alternatively, take Champagne, which is always well received.

Flowers can be tricky for dinner parties, as your host will have to find a vase and arrange the flowers when he or she often has more pressing things to do. You could always send flowers after the event. A lovely box of chocolates is another good standby (but please don't insist they are opened at the end of dinner), or, if your host is a bit of a foodie, take something for the kitchen like a bottle of good olive oil.

When to arrive

There are times when it's fine to be a bit late and there are times when punctuality matters, and common sense should dictate the difference. No matter how well you know your hosts, you should always be on time for dinner. If you are going to a barbeque or a tea, of course, timing is less crucial for your host and there is clearly some room for manoeuvre on your part.

If you have been told that dinner is eight for eight thirty, arriving a little after eight is about right. Don't arrive bang on eight, and definitely no earlier. Being very early is almost as bad as being late. Your host is probably dashing around laying the table, getting dressed or crying over a split sauce, and the last thing she needs is to entertain someone who has arrived an hour too soon. If you are unavoidably held up and going to be late, call ahead and let the host know roughly what time you will arrive. At least everyone else can start eating if they know you have been delayed.

THE PERFECT DINNER GUEST
DOS AND DON'TS

DO NOT DITCH invitations at the last minute without a watertight excuse. This is tricky if, for example, someone has just offered you a couple of tickets for an amazing concert or the object of your affections has finally asked you out on a hot date – only if you know your hosts well enough and are honest about what's come up can you hope that they will understand.

DO WAX LYRICAL about the food if it's good, but don't be too greedy. Your hosts will enjoy hearing you praise their wonderful cooking – but at the same time, remember that the apple and blackberry crumble in the middle of the table is meant for everyone, not just for you.

DO BE ENTERTAINING but don't subject everyone else to protracted tales of your troublesome boss/angelic toddlers/recent coach trip to the Dutch bulbfields. Good guests know how to talk and listen.

DON'T INSIST that other guests drink alcohol if they have already said they don't want to.

DO OFFER TO HELP clear up but do accept a polite refusal.

DO KNOW WHEN to go home even if you are having a great time. If your host is yawning loudly, determinedly clearing up around you or fast asleep, it is probably time to make a move.

The art of communication

Gone are the days when ladies of leisure spent mornings composing beautiful letters, invitations and thank-you notes. These days, the speed with which most of us communicate via phone, email and text message has made traditional forms of correspondence virtually redundant. However, for all their convenience, none of these fast means of communication comes close to the life-enhancing feeling of receiving a handwritten note, or the cosiness of sitting down and writing a long letter to a good friend.

Writing also provides the perfect excuse to spend some money on a lovely ink pen, thick paper and pretty tissue-lined envelopes. You can spend a few pounds on basic but good quality paper or several hundred pounds on hand-engraved personal stationery, but whichever you choose, it's good to remember that what you write on will speak volumes about you. From the most formal RSVPs through to short thank-you notes, correspondence should always be handwritten in blue or black ink, and never with messy biros, which make everything look like a note from the milkman. Coloured ink is sometimes appropriate, but colours can look cheap and tacky in the wrong context so use your judgement.

Try to keep a range of stationery at home or at work so you can write promptly and keep up with correspondence. Formal RSVPs should be written on blank or personal writing paper, while more informal notes and thank-yous can be written on correspondence cards or on vintage postcards.

Responding to invitations

If someone has been kind enough to invite you to something, whether it is an informal supper or a smart summer wedding, you should always reply as promptly as possible. It not only means that you will be organized and on top of things, but it is also polite to let your host know straight away if you are able to attend. Why should a bride have to chase up errant guests weeks before her wedding when she has a million and one other things to organize?

A good rule of thumb when replying to any invitation is that the reply should always be written with equal formality. If an invitation is written in the third person, as virtually all formal invitations are, your reply should also be written in the third person. Use blue or black ink and write on personal paper or plain writing paper and always reply to the RSVP address, which, in the case of a wedding, will usually be the bride's mother. There's no sign-off for third-person replies and the date goes in the bottom left-hand corner. Below are the formal ways to respond – adapt them to suit you.

For example:

Miss Arabella Hague thanks Mr and Mrs Thomas for their kind invitation to the wedding of their daughter Charlotte on Saturday, 14th June, and has great pleasure in accepting.

If you are unable to attend, then answer promptly confirming this and if possible state the reason why:

> *Miss Arabella Hague thanks Mr and Mrs Thomas*
> *for their kind invitation to the wedding of their*
> *daughter Charlotte on Saturday, 14th June, but*
> *regrets that she is unable to accept due to a*
> *previous engagement.*

If you accept an invitation and then find you are unable to attend, let your host know as soon as possible, and, if you know that you will be very much missed (if it's your god-daughter's wedding or your best friend's baby's christening, for example), send flowers too.

Thank-you notes

It is a rapidly disappearing courtesy but the thank-you note or letter is a fundamental of good etiquette, whether you are thanking for a simple supper at a friend's house, a long week-end in the country or even simply to show appreciation for some random kindness. A thoughtfully written thank-you is also lovely to receive and far better than getting a quickly thrown-together email or, worse, a text message (although of course it's better to hear something than nothing at all). Ideally, you should send a thank-you note within a few days, which also ensures that you keep up with correspondence, but even if you don't do it at once and it gets late, it's still worth bothering. Keep paper, cards and stamps stocked up so that you can write letters straight away – if you prefer to send cards or postcards then buy them in bulk when you see good ones; they will always come in useful.

If you find it difficult to write letters, don't try to be too formal. If you are sending a letter because you have been to a fun dinner party, then write about the food that you ate or a funny conversation to give your letter some colour. Gushing praise of your host (if deserved) is always a good idea too. Be friendly rather than stiff.

Condolence letters

A letter of condolence should be sent to the bereaved as soon as possible after a death; the sooner it is written, the more likely it is to sound sincere and heartfelt. Write it on rough paper initially if necessary, and don't get bogged down with what you think you should write or with clichéd comments.

What you write depends on how well you know the bereaved. If it is someone you are very close to, it will be much easier to write than to an aged relative with whom you have had little contact. You will probably empathize with the bereaved, so say so, and try to think of something positive to say about the deceased, even if it is a jolly story you remember that could bring a little short-term cheer.

Finally, condolence cards, which nearly always seem to feature some deeply depressing morbid flowers, are not always the most welcome things to receive. Write on personal paper or choose a card that you know will appeal to the bereaved – it could simply be something beautiful.

○ DO offer your help, perhaps with shopping or errands, but only if you mean it and are able to help.

○ DON'T be intrusive. Unless very close to the bereaved, it is wise to give them some space. Send a letter, and follow it up later with a telephone call.

○ DO wear respectful clothing to funerals. It is not mandatory to wear black to funerals these days, but stick to conservative colours unless the announcement states otherwise.

○ DO remember the bereaved after the funeral – especially around Christmas or anniversaries, when they might need extra support.

Introductions

Introducing people, whether in formal circumstances or when bumping into someone in the street, is an art, and when it is carried out confidently it makes a potentially awkward situation much less tricky. Always introduce succinctly and without fuss so that everyone feels at ease. If you are being introduced to someone make sure you make eye contact with them and offer a firm handshake, not a wimpy limp wrist. It's easy to forget names as soon as you have been introduced, but repeating names when you are introduced or during conversation is a good way to make sure the name sticks in your head. And if you can't remember, own up to your temporary amnesia.

○ DO state names clearly when making an introduction. Don't mumble or you will leave those being introduced confused.

○ DO try to give a bit of personal information when you are introducing two strangers at a party so they will have some talking points when you leave them alone.

○ DON'T panic if you forget someone's name just before making an introduction – start by saying something like 'Have you met before?' by which time they will probably offer their hand and say their name.

Weddings

Weddings are among the most formal events that any of us attend on a regular basis, and they seem to prompt more etiquette quandaries than any other occasion.

Traditionally details of the wedding list were never enclosed with the wedding invitation – the word was spread through family and friends. These days, however, as we all live at a more frantic pace, it is more convenient for many brides to send out everything together in one envelope. And anyone who has left gift-buying to the last minute will know that when it comes to the wedding list, it doesn't pay to delay. The longer you leave it the more chance there is that you will be left to choose between a set of tea towels, an ironing-board cover or some piece of electrical equipment that no one wants to be associated with, like a hedge strimmer. Now that many lists are also available on the internet, it makes the whole process incredibly simple, so there is no excuse for putting it off.

While it can be tempting to buy 'off-piste' so you can find something more personal, it is probably better to stick to things the couple have chosen, although if you know them very well and have something in mind you think they will love then that is slightly different. If you do decide to stray from the list, organize for your gift to be delivered to the bride or her mother ahead of the wedding day. Taking presents to the reception is an inconvenience for the bride, who will have to store them somewhere and then transport everything home. If you are buying from a list then all of this is taken care of.

WEDDING DOS AND DON'TS

DO NOT ASK to be invited to someone's wedding, and never ask if you can bring boyfriends or girlfriends if they have not been invited, unless it is a very obvious oversight.

DO THINK about what you are going to say before you come face to face with the receiving line at the wedding reception, but don't chat and hold up the line.

DO THANK the bride's parents before leaving the reception, and while it is not required, it is nice to send a note to thank the bride's parents after the wedding.

DO ALWAYS let the people in pews in front of you leave first when the ceremony is over.

DON'T CHAT during the service or during musical interludes, even if the Gregorian chant is boring you rigid.

Baby showers, births and christenings

Many women complain that as soon as their pregnancy is announced they are treated as public property. Virtual strangers think nothing of invading their body space and giving their bump an intrusive pat. So always bear in mind that when it comes to pregnancies, births and new babies, more tact than ever is required. Try to avoid making personal

Do TRY to arrive at the church at least fifteen minutes before the service is due to start. As well as being polite, this will also allow you to secure the best view from a good seat at the end of the pew. If you are late, enter the church quietly and inconspicuously.

Do NOT interfere with the seating plan at the wedding breakfast so you can sit near to friends or the man you've been flirting with all day.

DON'T rugby-tackle other female guests to try to catch the wedding bouquet. A well-planned jump is more elegant.

WHEN YOU ARRIVE at the church, do not seat yourself or you could end up in the wrong place. Families get very territorial at these occasions. The ushers will take you to your seat once they have ascertained your relationship to the bride or groom.

comments about how big/small the bump is or how dreadful your best friend's sister's labour was. Would you want to hear in-depth accounts of horrific labour just months or weeks before stepping into the unknown? Also, no matter how tempting, try not to comment on the name that has been chosen for a new or soon-to-be-born baby – no matter how hilarious you might think the name is, it's not your place to comment or criticize what was probably a long and well-thought-out decision.

Baby showers

This American export has finally made it to our shores, thanks to a rash of celebrity baby showers, but there are a lot of good reasons to throw a shower for your closest friends. Traditionally held about a month before the due date, the baby shower is not only a good way to make sure the mother-to-be has everything she needs, it's also a good opportunity for a group of friends to gather together and show some support. The trans-Atlantic versions can be gilt-edged affairs that boast the best party planners, florists and caterers in town, but it's just as much fun to organize an afternoon where the emphasis is on morale-boosting enjoyment – a kind of Alice in Wonderland tea party with cute gifts and gorgeous cakes, say. A big advantage of a tea party for the mother-to-be is that she wouldn't have been able to drink alcohol in any case, so indulgent tea and cakes are the best alternative.

Births

In the excitement of one of your friends having had a baby, it is very tempting to rush along to congratulate the new parents, but think carefully before you do. Even if you have been invited to go round, it is often better to wait a few weeks for the furore to die down and to give them a chance to catch their breath. It is easier to send a card and arrange a visit at a later date, and if you want to send flowers then check how long the mother and baby are going to be in hospital or wait until they have got home before sending them, though obviously this depends on how close you are to the parents.

BABY SHOWER TIPS

from Tamara Mellon, MD of Jimmy Choo

ASK A COUPLE of your best friends to 'host' the party for you. This will usually include organizing the guest-list, catering and decoration.

TO MAKE IT EASIER, throw a themed party, such as a pampering party at a day spa, or a tea at home with close friends. I had iced tea, Champagne and Mimosa, little cakes, crudités and a cheese platter. To decorate we used big bunches of white flowers with silver and cream balloons.

YOU CAN ORGANIZE some games, too, such as guessing the baby's weight or date of birth, and then have a prize for whoever guesses correctly when the time comes.

GIFTS SHOULD INCLUDE must-haves to help you arrange the nursery. I asked friends who had already had a baby to bring something that they found extremely useful which they were given for their baby shower. It is helpful to have a registry so that your friends can avoid duplications. They could also club together for one bigger gift too.

I GAVE MY GUESTS goody bags with Jo Malone candles, Janet Reger underwear, small bouquets and silk print Jimmy Choo mules. Obviously it doesn't need to be as elaborate as this, but party favours are a must.

While you are not obliged to send a gift when a new baby is born, most close friends and family do. Alternatively, buy something for the new mother, who is probably drowning in cute toys and baby clothes by this point and would appreciate some indulgent gift for herself. Buy her a voucher to have a beauty treatment or pedicure at home (there are lots of companies that now offer home visits) or do a little hamper of gorgeous body products and oils.

Traditionally godparents were on hand to offer a child spiritual guidance, but these days the role of the godparents, selected from close family and friends, is no longer always as devout as this. However, whether or not you are religious, it is still a serious undertaking, and there is little point in accepting the role if you are unable to celebrate birthdays and keep in touch. If you do not want to take on the responsibility because you already have a number of godchildren or for any other reason, it is perfectly acceptable to politely refuse.

Godparents should choose a christening gift that will stand the test of time. These include silver mugs and nursery gifts, or something that will be useful in later life such as precious books or a savings account (which can be boosted at each birthday). Laying down some wine is an alternative, and one that will make you very popular when your godchild comes of age. Girls can be given jewellery – a cross and chain is traditional but charm bracelets are also a good idea as these can be added to throughout life.

Dress codes

IT'S TOUGH ENOUGH PLANNING what to wear each day in the normal run of things, but when faced with an event some of us are thrown into a frenzy of anxiety. Why is getting dressed such a drama? These days, dress codes have become confusingly blurred. Jeans are worn to everything from cocktail parties to black tie events yet they wouldn't get you past the revolving doors of the Ritz. While we live in a persistently

---

SOME BASIC POINTERS ON GETTING DRESSED

AVOID wearing new shoes to any event, but especially one where you will be standing for long periods or dancing. Wear them in first, or remember to take a few blister plasters in your handbag.

ALWAYS get the right underwear for your party clothes. Obvious straps, visible lines and badly fitting lingerie will ruin your look, no matter how much of a killer outfit you have put together.

JEWELLERY is a great instant lift for party clothes but be careful not to overdo it. If your clothes are plain it is fine to wear bold jewels, but if you are wearing prints or ornate clothes then wear only simple jewels.

dress-down culture, there are still clubs where the sharpest dressers in exquisite bespoke suits will be ejected for not wearing a tie. And while some women do anything to avoid wearing a gown, other quirky souls decide to wear a party dress to go shopping in the middle of the day. No matter how undefined these boundaries are, the important thing to remember here is that some people can get away with doing their own thing, while the rest of us probably can't. If you wear clothes with confidence you can get away with pretty much anything (nonchalance is usually the only accessory you need to get beyond the velvet rope), but when it comes to rigid dress codes – and these do exist in a handful of places – it is always best to play by the rules.

Most important is to make an effort – it is a harsh fact of life that first impressions count, and whether or not we like this we all know that on slovenly days when we can't be bothered to do our hair or get dressed up, the world responds to us in a totally different way. Yet with glossy hair, glowing skin and smart clothes we miraculously become the most admired person in the room – or at least it sometimes feels that way.

There are the things a girl can't go wrong with. No matter how boring it seems, the little black dress will take you virtually anywhere. Whenever you chance upon a perfect black cocktail dress, buy it – a glamorous LBD is timeless, elegant and flattering. Equally, well-cut simple shift dresses in most colours can be upgraded with jewellery and heels for most parties. If dresses aren't your thing, then invest in a tuxedo suit in black or, more interestingly, midnight blue;

women look fabulous in these slick, masculine jackets and they are a great idea for anyone who steers clear of girly frocks. If you are in a panic about any party, keeping everything as simple as possible is usually the best game plan. Elegant separates – a plain silk tank with well-cut trousers or a long straight skirt – is just as smart as a dress and probably easier to wear too.

Of course, dress codes for women are more open to interpretation than dress codes for men, but if you are going to an event you have never been to before and you want to wear the right thing, always check with a few friends who have been before, or call the organizers to gauge the degree of formality.

White tie

Reserved for the glitziest receptions (and, of course, Elton John parties), white tie is as formal as it gets, but at least this means the rules are clear. For women: a full-length evening dress, small silk evening bag and evening shoes, and piles of jewels. For men: black tail coat, matching black trousers – traditionally with two rows of braid down the side seam, white Marcella waistcoat and shirt with studs and detachable wing collar, white Marcella bow tie and black patent pumps or shoes.

Black tie

Black tie has become a hazy dress code in some circles, and you will need to use common sense or do some research to gauge just how formal your event is. But black tie could mean anything from a long dress for very smart parties or dinners to a shorter cocktail dress or even trousers with a dressy top. A good modern alternative for formal black-tie events is to wear a long silk skirt with a short-sleeved cashmere top. For men black tie is straightforward: black wool dinner jacket, matching trousers, sometimes with one row of braid down the side seam, black waistcoat or a black cummerbund, cotton or silk shirt with soft turn-down collar, black silk bow tie, black shoes and black socks.

Morning dress

Worn by men for the smartest weddings and for some events during the Season, morning dress can either be in black or grey. For Royal Ascot and some other events a grey top hat is worn and sometimes a grey three-piece morning suit. Top hats are always removed indoors and the jacket should never be unbuttoned except when sitting down, when coat tails should be flipped over the back of the chair. Black morning dress consists of: black morning coat, striped grey wool trousers, a plain waistcoat that can be single- or double-breasted, a dress shirt with a separate white collar, silver tie, black patent or leather lace-up shoes, black top hat.

Smart casual

The most dreaded dress code of all. Not only is it utterly vague but it also implies that were there not a dress code we would all turn up in towelling tracksuits. It is safe to assume that so long as you have made an effort you can wear pretty much anything.

Dressing for weddings

What to wear to a wedding will depend on where the wedding is and what time of day it is – for example, while it is easy for most of us to dress for a summer wedding in the English countryside, it might be less obvious what to wear to an evening wedding in New York. If in doubt you should ask the bride's mother, who will know exactly what degree of formality is expected. If morning dress is stipulated, then all men must wear morning suits, not just the wedding party, and women should wear day suits or dresses with or without hats.

○ DO take something to cover up with if you are wearing a strappy dress. Bare shoulders, décolleté and too much exposed flesh is not a good look at a wedding, even if it's a civil ceremony.

○ DO try to avoid wearing black. While it has become more acceptable for women to wear black at weddings, it is much nicer to wear pretty colours – especially in the summer.

○ DO take the opportunity to dress up. Even if your friends are not wearing hats, don't feel that you shouldn't either.

○ DO trade a hat for a headdress or ornate band for an evening wedding. Hats seem too formal for ceremonies held late in the day, and you can keep smaller bands and pins on all evening.

○ DO always check what to wear to a wedding
abroad. Dress codes vary widely in different
countries and you don't want to feel out of place
when you are a long way from home and
surrounded by strangers.

Specific events

Once upon a time the summer season was the domain of the
upper classes, the well connected and the seriously wealthy.
Now that the same events rely on the deep pockets of corpo-
rate entertainers, things are quite different. Anyone can now
find themselves gambling at Royal Ascot, or, even better,
spending an evening at Glyndebourne. But while the guests
may have changed (often radically), the dress codes in most
cases haven't. Some old rules are still rigorously enforced and
in many places you will be turned away for wearing inappro-
priate clothes, so it's always advisable to check, and also
remember that codes vary according to which enclosure you
are in.

Royal Ascot

In the Royal Enclosure, women have to wear formal day dress,
which can be a summer dress or a suit – trouser suits are now
allowed. Hats that cover the crown of the head must be worn
for the Royal Enclosure, although elaborate feathered bands
or headdresses on little caps are increasingly acceptable. The
dressiest day is Ladies Day, traditionally held on the Thursday.
Men wear morning dress with a top hat, which can be black or

grey. While the dress code is much less rigid for the grandstand, most women wear formal day dress with hats, while men wear everything from morning dress through to cool summer suits. No jeans, shorts or trainers are allowed.

Henley Royal Regatta
In the steward's enclosure, women should wear dresses or skirts that cover their knees, and no trousers or culottes are permitted. It is not obligatory to wear a hat, although many guests do. Men wear lounge suits or blazers with a shirt and tie and flannels, and many men also wear a boater or panama hat. No jeans, shorts, T-shirts trainers or sandals are permitted.

Cartier International Polo
There is no enforced dress code for the Cartier Polo, although most women choose to wear long, cool summer dresses while men wear light summer suits. Some women choose to wear hats, although they are not obligatory.

Glyndebourne Festival Opera and other smart opera festivals
Although most guests at Glyndebourne wear black tie, as long as guests are smart they would be admitted. Women wear long or short evening dresses or smart trouser suits. No jeans, shorts, T-shirts trainers or sandals are permitted.

The Directory

WHERE CAN YOU GET A TIN WATERING CAN, send your antique napkins for cleaning or find one hundred pink roses at a bargain price? This directory contains telephone numbers, and websites where applicable, for all the companies mentioned throughout the book. There are also a few notable firms thrown in for good measure, with additional notes of explanation. This is not an exhaustive list but rather a source-book of useful places. Thanks to the internet and mail order, no matter where you live you will have access to virtually all the companies listed here. At the end are a few numbers that should prove useful for emergencies.

Wardrobes

Muji: 020 7323 2208 for branches nationwide; *www.muji.co.uk*; mail order

Morplan: 0800 451122; *www.morplan.com*; mail order

The Holding Company: 020 8445 2888; *www.theholdingcompany.co.uk*; mail order

Ikea: 08453 551141; *www.ikea.co.uk*

Paperchase: 0161 839 1500; *www.paperchase.co.uk*; mail order

Cashmere Clinic: 9 Beauchamp Place, London SW3; 020 7584 9806

John Lewis: 08456 049050; *www.johnlewis.co.uk*; mail order

KG Shoes: 020 7387 2234 or go to *www.cobbler.co.uk*; postal service

Mayfair Cobblers: 4 White Horse Street, London W1; 020 7491 3426; postal service

Chelsea Green Shoe Repair: 31 Elystan Street, London SW3; 020 7584 0776

The Bedroom

Brora: 020 7736 9944; *www.brora.co.uk*; mail order

Toast: 0870 240 5200; *www.toastbypost.co.uk*; mail order

Hush: 020 7622 3725; *www.hush-uk.com*; mail order

Californian Closets: 241–245 King's Road, London SW3; 020 8208 4544; *www.calclosets.com*

Red Flower: at Harvey Nichols, Knightsbridge, London SW1, 020 7235 5000; 21 New Cathedral Street, Manchester, 0161 828 8888; 107–111 Briggate, Leeds, 0113 204 8888; The Mailbox, 31–32 Wharfside, Birmingham, 0121 616 6000; 30–34 St Andrews Square, Edinburgh; 0131 524 8388

L'Artisan Parfumeur: 17 Cale Street, London SW3; 020 7352 4196; mail order

Body Shop: 01903 731 500 for stores nationwide

House of Fraser: 08701 607270; *www.hof.co.uk*. One of the best high-street department stores for bedding and bedlinen.

Cabbages and Roses: 53 Ledbury Road, London W11; 020 7034 0008; *www.cabbagesandroses.com*; mail order. Beautiful vintage-inspired fabrics, bedlinens, old-fashioned eiderdowns, traditional deckchairs and other homey accessories.

Cath Kidston: 51 Marylebone High Street, W1; 020 7935 6555; *www.cathkidston.co.uk*; mail order. Pretty, retro accessories including table linen, crockery, bathroom bits and bobs and, of course, ironing-board covers.

Cologne and Cotton: 74 Regent's Street, Leamington Spa, Warwickshire; 01926 881485; *www.cologneandcotton.com*; mail order. A great catalogue for traditional satin-trimmed wool blankets, mohair throws, fluffy Turkish towels and robes.

The Bathroom

The White Company: 12 Marylebone High Street, London W1, 020 7823 5322; 15 Northgate Street, Bath, 01225 445 284; 52 George Street, Edinburgh, 0131 225 2991; 0870 900 9555, *www.thewhitecompany.com* for additional stockists and mail order. Great source for bedlinen, towels and good-looking bathroom accessories.

Aquis towels: 020 8735 2882

Space NK: Knightsbridge, London SW1; 020 7201 8636; *www.spacenk.co.uk*

Bliss Spa: 60 Sloane Avenue, London SW3; 020 7584 3888; *www.blissworld.com*; mail order

Fenwick: 63 New Bond Street, London W1; 020 7629 9161

Neal's Yard Remedies: 020 7627 1949;
www.nealsyardremedies.com; mail order

REN: 0845 2255600; *www.renskincare.com*; mail order

Aromatherapy Associates: 020 8569 7030;
www.aromatherapyassociates.com; mail order

B&Q: 08456 096 688 for stores nationwide

V Aslotel Ltd: 01372 362 533; mail order

Liz Earle: 01983 813 913; *www.lizearle.com*; mail order

Jo Malone: 01730 232 411; *www.jomalone.co.uk*; mail order

Laundry

Durance en Provence by The French Company: 01728
603310; mail order

L'Occitane: stockist enquiry number 020 7907 0301;
mail order

Roberts Radio: 01709 571722; *www.robertsradio.co.uk*.
Old-fashioned radios in the most delicious colours.

Blossom and Browne's Sycamore Laundry: 020 8552 1231;
www.blossomandbrowne.com; postal service

N. Peal: 37 Burlington Arcade, London W1; 020 7493 5378;
www.npeal.com

Housework

Association of Art and Antique Dealers: 020 7823 3511;
www.lapada.co.uk

Antiquax chandelier and crystal spray: 0870 908 9327;
mail order

Diptyque: 195 Westbourne Grove, London W11;
020 7727 8673; mail order

McQueens Florist: 126 St John's Street, London EC1;
020 7251 5505; *www.mcqueens.co.uk*

New Covent Garden Flower Market: Covent House,
London SW8; *www.cgma.gov.uk*; Mon–Fri 3a.m. until
11a.m.; Sat 4a.m. until 10a.m. Entry is £4 per vehicle; free if
you are on foot. If you are planning to fill your house with
flowers for a party or need to buy any kind of flower, plant
or pot in bulk, this is the place to come. This is where florists
come to buy so prices are way below the high street. The best
time to come is early on a Thursday.

Graham and Green: 10 Elgin Crescent, London W11; 0870
044 5656 and *www.grahamandgreen.co.uk* for mail order.
Gorgeous mirrors, glass ceramics and loungewear at the
Notting Hill shop, a smaller selection of which is available
via mail order.

The Kitchen

Lakeland: 015394 88100; *www.lakelandlimited.com*;
mail order

Cucina Direct: 0870 420 4311; *www.cucinadirect.co.uk*;
mail order

Le Creuset: 0800 373792; *www.lecreuset.com.uk*; mail order
available from Elizabeth David Cook Shop, 22 Fitzroy Street,
Cambridge, 01223 321579

David Mellor Cutlery: The Round Building, Heathersage;
01433 650220; *www.davidmellordesign.co.uk*; mail order

Divertimenti: 33–34 Marylebone High Street, London W1;
020 7935 0689; *www.divertimenti.co.uk*; mail order

John Lewis: 08456 049049; *www.johnlewis.co.uk*; mail order

Kenwood: 01239 247 6000; *www.kenwood.co.uk*

Baileys Home and Garden: The Engine Shed, Station
Approach, Ross-on-Wye, Herefordshire; 01989 561 931;
www.baileyshomeandgarden.com; mail order. Brilliant shop
and catalogue full of new and second-hand kitchen and
home wares, including butler's sinks, laundry accessories and
gardening tools.

KitchenAid: 00800 381 04026 and available mail order
through *www.johnlewis.co.uk*. This is the food mixer you
want to have standing in your kitchen. It's not necessarily
any more efficient than the excellent mixers by Kenwood but
the colours and retro shape are irresistible.

Skandium: 86 Marylebone High Street, London W1; 020 7935 2077. Cool Scandinavian fabrics, ceramics and other home wares, but best of all are the Iittala pressed-glass Marimekko bowls, which come in all colours of the rainbow and are perfect for filling with ice-cream sundaes, berries and piles of sweets.

Cooking

The Soil Association: 0117 929 0661; *www.soilassociation.org*

Northfield Farm: 01664 474271; *www.northfieldfarm.com*; also at Borough Market, London SE1 every Friday and Saturday; mail order

Swaddles: 0845 456 1768; *www.swaddles.co.uk*; mail order

Wild Meat Company: 01728 663211; *www.wildmeat.co.uk*; mail order

Graig Farm: 01597 851655; *www.graigfarm.co.uk*; mail order

Neal's Yard Dairy: 6 Park Street, Borough Market, London SE1; 020 7645 3550; *www.nealsyarddairy.com*; mail order

Paxton and Whitfield: 3 John Street, Bath; 01225 466 403; 93 Jermyn Street, London SW1; 020 7930 0259; *www.paxtonandwhitfield.co.uk*; mail order

La Fromagerie: 30 Highbury Park, London N5; 020 7359 7440; *www.lafromagerie.co.uk*

Entertaining

Coco London: 0870 7522590; *www.cocolondon.com*

Konditor and Cook: 22 Cornwall Road, London SE1; 020 7261 0456; limited mail order nationwide

Ottolenghi: 63 Ledbury Road, London W11; 020 7727 1121

Ladurée: 16 rue Royale, Paris 75008; 00 33 1 42 60 21 79. One of the best patisseries in Paris and the place to stock up on the prettiest macaroons in town. Buy in bulk and take home for tea parties. As a bonus they come packaged in the most divine celadon-green card boxes. The salted caramel bonbons are also mind-blowingly good.

Pot Luck: Columbia Road, London, E1; 020 7722 6892; open Friday 10a.m.–3p.m.; Sunday 8a.m.–2.30p.m.

Berry Bros and Rudd: 3 St James's Street, London SW1; 0870 900 4300; mail order

L'Artisan du Chocolat: 89 Lower Sloane Street, London SW3; 020 7824 8365; mail order

The Chocolate Society: 36 Elizabeth Street, London SW1; 020 7259 9222; mail order 01423 322238

Pierre Marcolini: 6 Lancer Square, London W8; 020 7795 6611; mail order

Majestic Wine Warehouses: 0845 605 6767; *www.majestic.co.uk*

Oddbins: 0800 328 2323; *www.oddbins.com*

Adnams: Victoria Street, Southwold, Suffolk; 01502 727222; *www.adnams.co.uk*; mail order. Brewery has good selection of wine available by mail order (and still delivers local orders on a horse and cart). There is also a good cookshop at the Southwold shop.

Etiquette

Smythson: 40 New Bond Street, London W1; 020 7318 1515; mail order

RK Alliston: 6 Quiet Street, Bath; 173 New King's Road, Parson's Green, London SW6; 0845 130 5577; *www.rkalliston.com*; mail order

Non Stop Party Shop: www.nonstopparty.co.uk; 020 7937 7200

Confetti: 80–81 Tottenham Court Road, London W1; 0870 7747171; *www.confetti.co.uk*

Farmacia Santa Maria Novella: 117 Walton Street, London SW3; 020 7460 6600; mail order

Really useful numbers

British Gas: for billing and other information call 0845 600 5100; *www.house.co.uk*. But for emergencies and suspected gas leaks call Transco: 0800 111999; *www.transco.co.uk*

British Pest Control Association: 01332 294288; *www.bpca.org.uk*

National Association of Chimney Sweeps: 01785 811732/0800 833464; *www.chimneyworks.co.uk*

Electrical Contractors Association: 020 7313 4800; *www.eca.co.uk*; for lists of affiliated electricians nationwide

Master Locksmiths Association: 0800 783 1498; *www.locksmiths.co.uk*; for lists of affiliated locksmiths nationwide

Institute of Plumbing: 01708 472 791; *www.plumbers.org.uk*; for lists of affiliated plumbers nation-wide, as well as practical advice on plumbing and what to do in emergencies

Federation of Master Builders: 020 7242 7583; *www.findabuilder.co.uk*; for lists of affiliated builders, as well as practical advice on avoiding cowboys.

RSPCA: 0870 5555 999; *www.rspca.org.uk*

Acknowledgements

First and foremost a huge thank you to the wonderful Paul Davies at the *Daily Telegraph* for his encouragement, wise words and never-ending, super-human patience. This book wouldn't have got off the ground without his help and would certainly never have been completed. I'd also like to thank Derren Gilhooley for his boundless enthusiasm, constant reassurance and fabulous ideas. Many friends have been so supportive but I owe special thanks to Angela Brown, Gill Christophers, Georgina Cover, Malika Dalamal, Paula Fitzherbert, Rachel Meddowes, Krishna Montgomery, Charlotte Pennington, Paul Raeside, Nikki Wellspring, Paul White, Melissa Whitworth, Libby Willis and Nicky Yates. I am really grateful to all the experts who have contributed to this book and to their publicists who helped extract the information. I would also like to thank my agent, Kate Jones at ICM, and Selina Walker, Cora Kipling and everyone at Transworld.

Index